Recovering
Catholics

Recovering
Catholics

*What to Do When Religion
Comes Between You and God*

Earnie Larsen
and **Janee Parnegg**

HarperSanFrancisco
A Division of HarperCollins*Publishers*

FIRST EDITION

Library of Congress Cataloging-in-Publication Data

Larsen, Earnest. Recovering Catholics : what to do when religion comes between you and God / Earnie Larsen and Janee Parnegg. — 1st ed.
p. cm.
Includes bibliographical references.
ISBN 0–06–064955–0
1. Church work with ex-church members—Catholic Church.
2. Reconciliation—Religious aspects—Catholic Church.
3. Authority (Religion) 4. Control (Psychology)—Religious aspects—
Christianity. I. Parnegg, Janee. II. Title.
BX2347.8.E82L37   1992   91–58903
248.4'82—dc20   CIP

92   93   94   95   96   M-V   10   9   8   7   6   5   4   3   2   1

This edition is printed on acid-free paper that meets the American
National Standards Institute Z39.48 Standard.

To Jack Boland, my friend, mentor, example,
who knows the way "it really is."
E. L.

To Bishop George E. Bates,
a true companion and loving guide on the spiritual path,
and to Fr. Lyman E. Howard, whose life is a beacon
shining through his own suffering with such joy.
J. P.

Contents

Preface

*R*ecovering Catholics comes from a heart that loves the church and from a belief that for all the crimes, faults, and failings of religion, on the whole religion's impact on humanity has been more positive than negative. In fact, for many, the church is the single most important lifeline to what Jesus called "the abundant life."

I was born into a Catholic family, became an altar boy, spent nine years of preparation before being ordained a priest, and served the church in that capacity for thirteen years. Thankfully, I am one of the relatively few resigned priests who has received formal dispensation from my vows from Rome, a process called *laicization*. Besides loving the church, I am also a committed member of my parish community. And it is because of this love and commitment that I write these pages.

What follows is meant to express my ardent hope and belief that the church as an institution has not only an opportunity but an urgent responsibility to speak ever more authentically to the hearts of contemporary human beings. This opportunity must not be allowed to pass when bold, in-depth leadership is so desperately needed.

Recovering Catholics is humbly written to raise important questions and encourage openness—constantly improving the quality of the call that invites each and all to that greater depth and blazing light where God stands beckoning.

I hope the attitude revealed throughout these pages will be apparent. Janee Parnegg and I don't mean to judge who is the "good guy" and who is the "bad." Our staunchly held belief is that pain is basically for the birds! Pain hurts, and most human beings, by and large, have had too much pain in their lives.

Second, we don't believe that God deliberately wills people to have pain. God does not put pain into people's lives in order to test them, teach them a lesson, or—worst of all—because it gives God pleasure to watch people suffer. We believe that when pain comes into our lives, whether it is self-induced or not, God's passionate desire is that we allow our healing by being open to the power of the divine. God's thing is human well-being.

Negative religious experiences hurt. In fact, little in the endless catalog of human misery hurts more than being abandoned, betrayed, or punished by those in whom we have put our trust. When we ask for bread and receive a stone, the ultimate dirty trick has been played!

We know that a great many have been hurt in just this manner. We have met them. Betrayal at the hands of other people is bad enough, but when we feel betrayed by God, it is catastrophic. After all, people are just people—we know they are full of faults. But God! If we think God has withdrawn or has cast us away, then how shall we ever find a fire to warm us? If the source of all love and goodness turns away from us, what hope can there be to find the peace and serenity for which our hearts so yearn?

We hope this book will draw clear, distinct lines between frequently confusing and overlapping concepts—such as the difference between religion (full of flawed humanity) and God (who is not). It is our fierce desire to help people who feel that God has abandoned them to look with different eyes, to think with a different mentality, to approach with an open heart the question of just who this God might be—or better, who God might be *to them.*

It is our intention to offer a healing balm to soothe the burning anger, to help straighten twisted thinking, to revive broken hope. God is never lost to us. There is always a way back to God, and it is never too late either to find God or deepen the relationship that has been there all along.

Into this wide net fall different sorts of people:

Those who have been hurt by religion and have abandoned God.

We ask you to consider again the source of your pain and the consequences you deal yourself by blurring the distinctions between God and religion. They are not the same. An unhappy or unhealthy cleric who mistreated you decades ago was not God. The faults, failures, and at times out-and-out sins of the church are not God either. Nor are all those examples of misguided or downright prejudiced dogma that have been put forth from time to time by the "church God." In fact, there may well be no greater "proof" for the existence of God than the fact that, despite all the failures and human dullness exhibited by the church through the ages, it still exists and is still capable, for all its shortcomings, of playing a positive role in the human drama.

To you we say, think again. Consider reaching out to God, whether you have abandoned all religion, tried another denomination, or simply figured that you have to walk the road alone. Whatever path you may have chosen, God is here, God is love, and God loves you.

Those who have been hurt by religion, and have remained "in" but unmoved.

To you we also say, think again. God is not religion. God is the verb that has the answers, knows the secrets, and can make a mighty difference in your life. Compliance is not the same as commitment. Religious compliance without the inner life is like baking a delicious pie but never taking a piece for yourself.

As we will point out in the following pages, the key to all real relationships with God is a personal, soul-converting meeting with the God who would—and does—move heaven and earth for you if only you would open the door! When God becomes personal, God becomes real. Not before. When God becomes personal, it won't matter if the medieval popes sired children or sold indulgences, or if some small-minded priest or nun humiliated you. It won't matter if the weekly homily leaves you unfed and saddened about wasting such valuable time on trivialities. What will matter a lot is that when God becomes personal you will become motivated to get involved in the church community, to stir up a little fire.

People are all so different. We are all on our unique journeys toward God and with God, though it all may seem a bit fuzzy at times. God is bigger than any thought about God; God is more profound than any package of dogma and ritual officially sanctioned by the church. Yet God is also the simplest of realities. God is as simple as a breeze whispering to your heart, as simple as the deeply penetrating reality of—"Fear not. It is I. I am here, so there is nothing to worry about."

For human beings who get so terribly tangled in so many confusing webs, this is about as simple as it gets: I am here. I love you. Let's do it together.

Simple works. God works. Our goal for you, however it plays out, is let it work!

Recovering
Catholics

• 1 •

Has Religion Come Between You and God?

An individual's quest for God—let alone a nation or a world seeking the kiss of the Divine—is matched in difficulty only by its importance. Obstacles constantly seem to block the path, obstacles as complex as the workings of the human mind as it gropes toward God and as varied as the endless nuances by which people experience their lives.

Strange as it may seem, religion, or more precisely, one's past experience of religion, has become for many not the golden stairway to God but precisely one of those spirit-jarring obstacles. For all the energy, time, stress, and pageantry demanded by most religions, notwithstanding the warm secure feelings past religious experiences may have generated, large numbers of sincere, dedicated folk have found religion on the whole to be a wall between them and the God with whom they so dearly seek communion.

There is a most touching image in the Book of Genesis where the author depicts what God has in mind for humankind and how people operate best. In this passage, God is strolling in the garden in the cool of the evening, calling out to Adam, "Where are you?"

Walking with God as a friend in the cool of the evening . . . how terribly appealing in this stress-ravaged, guilt-ridden, pressure-cooker existence that most of us call life. If only, our hearts sigh desperately, if only we could find that gentle face of God in this cruel world. If only we could capture an abiding sense of dwelling in the shadow of an all-loving, all-caring Presence, who somehow (with the magic only God could know) would reach across the chasm called death and rearrange the pieces of this crazy wasteful, sorrowful world with a divine alchemy, ultimately making sense out of nonsense. How wonderful that would be!

This is what millions crave. A walk in the cool of the evening with their God. Maybe even telling a joke or two, swapping stories, finding out "how's it going with you?" . . . just confidently, lovingly resting with one another, being with one another, knowing God cares.

It doesn't seem too much to ask. It is, in fact, the task religion is supposed to make happen. So what are the multitudes to think—to do—when they come to realize, that for them, instead of a walk in the cool of the evening, their past religious experience has made it a traffic jam in hell. Or if not quite that, it has certainly provided some serious potholes along the avenue of the Divine.

Blaming, of course, is as useless as idle complaining while your house burns down. Complaining doesn't put out fires. Blaming doesn't protect our precious possessions from the flames. And certainly griping and grousing years after some tragedy occurred is a total waste of life. Even if something took place that "should not have happened," if it did, then it did. To allow resentment and rage to fill our hearts is tantamount to setting our hearts and spirits aflame each new day. No one loses but ourselves. No one's life is left the poorer but our own.

When All Else Fails

Recently, I watched a young married man and his father put together a wedding present whose box clearly read, "some assembly required." The gift was a grill. There were dozens of parts in plastic bags containing hundreds of screws, belts, widgets, and springs. The young man dug right in with all the confidence of youth. The father, with that tone of irritated fondness many fathers of young adult sons seem to use, said, "Read the directions, son. They didn't print them just to have something to do. If you'll just read the directions, you'll save yourself thousands of hours of frustration!" It was obvious he was a veteran of many "some assembly required" projects. Sure enough, it wasn't too long before the younger man was scratching his head, searching for the instructions. When all else fails, follow the directions!

Although any human attempt to compile a set of directions on how to find God is bound to fall far short of the mark, there are some rules that if not understood, will surely make the journey more difficult. A critical fact for those embedded in religion, or who have had problems with religion, is that *God is not religion*.

When we make religion God, as sure as night follows day, frustration and confusion will follow. Religion is flawed. Religious people are far from perfect. Customs surrounding religion change. Forms of sacraments are subject to radical revision. Perceptions of dogma ebb and flow constantly over the centuries.

To make God one with religion is to run the risk that as religion is found to be flawed, and/or some of those religious people we hold in high esteem are found to have feet of clay, or worse, to be downright sinners (perhaps much worse than we have ever been ourselves!), we either totally discard God right along with our religion, or we simply lose faith in both.

Tragically, there are many people who find it traumatic even to enter a church today because of their sense of abuse at the hand of organized religion. More often than not, and this is the critical issue, these people bemoan their sorrow at thus having to live without God.

Why?

God is not bound by a set of circumstances. God is more than dogma, more than theology about God, and certainly more than the frail human vessels carrying the Word who is God to the best of their ability, whether we consider that ability to be adequate or not.

Miss this basic principle and the loss can be catastrophic in one's searching for God. How many heartrending ways this confusion has been voiced.

"Recovering Catholic"

"Hi! My name is Kathleen. I'm an alcoholic and a recovering Catholic."

As this introduction is made repeatedly at various Twelve-Step meetings around the country, knowing smiles light up some faces while expressions of bewilderment appear on others. Even more mystifying, this topic is no longer confined to recovery group meeting rooms. It has become coffee break conversation or lunch time sharing; references to having a Catholic or some other religious upbringing sometimes is heard on the cocktail and dinner party circuit. Books, movies, and television specials have surely made hay on the topic!

By now, many folks are pretty sure what the term *alcoholic* (or codependent or adult child) means, but what on earth does *recovering Catholic* mean? (Or, for that matter, anyone in any other denomination.) Recovering from what?

Anyone within shouting distance of middle age who was brought up in the Roman Catholic church has vivid memories about the church of yesterday, which, for the most part, by the way, no longer exists.

DELIGHTFUL MEMORIES

In the past twenty or thirty years, many books have been written about growing up in the Catholic church. Some are rather nostalgic and describe such things as patent leather shoes, and nine first Fridays (receiving Communion on the first Friday of nine consecutive months, so that if you died you would go straight to heaven), the smell of incense, the organ pounding out the "Tantum Ergo," and the sweet mystical sound of sanctus bells.

A twinkling Irishman regaled his listeners with a story about a high school prom at good old St. Mary's, when everyone was expected to call at the convent before the dance began as a sign of respect for the sisters. Of course, everyone knew that the nuns really wanted to make sure that the girls' formals weren't cut too low. With a devilish grin, he described the demure little shawls that most of the girls wore when they presented themselves at the convent, only to chuck them at the door of the dance hall.

It almost seems that among some older, still very active Catholics, there is a sort of jolly contest to see who can come up with the most outrageous stories: about old Sister Mary Agnes and how mean she was, or the time you were an altar boy and forgot to light the altar candles. Boy, did Father Raymond give it to you then! All this is told with ample relish, delight, lots of laughter, reverence, and respect. These memories are important and cherished parts of their lives. For some reason, they have been able to keep the good and leave the bad.

AND TERRIBLE MEMORIES

For others, it is a very different story. A young woman expressed deep sadness because she had remarried and could no longer be part of the church she had loved. After several conferences with her parish priest, she felt caught between spending the rest of her life alone, or having a loving, responsible relationship. She chose the latter and now feels, in deep pain, that she stands outside the church's embrace.

Their name is legion, longing for what they knew as children; the beauty and safety, the warm, wonderful memories of midnight Mass at Christmas, the agony of confession followed by the joy of feeling brand new, clean and free. Now, because of some happening in their life—perhaps the use of birth control, or an abortion, or a divorce—they see themselves as excluded from their spiritual home.

There are others, too full of rage and hostility to remember the good because for them there was so little of it. They are unable to let go of the bad because it seems to stick like napalm, the memories dogging their steps, scorching every single day of their lives. Their experience of growing up Catholic has left them with an abiding sense of guilt, shame, and anger. They find what was done to them in the name of God and religion absolutely unacceptable and completely inexcusable.

Across the lunch table at a quiet little restaurant, a woman in her early fifties described her last pregnancy. It was hard to imagine this chic, vibrant female as exhausted and ill, carrying her sixth child in almost the same number of years. "I can still remember the feeling, a sort of sick shameful anger that went all over me when it hit me that if it came right down to it, they would save the baby and let me die." Tears welled up in her eyes, her voice choked to a whisper. "There I was in labor, wondering what would happen to my other five children . . . the church sure as hell wouldn't mother them. . ." She went on to describe an enormous sense of betrayal and abandonment by the church she had tried so hard to serve. "It finally dawned on me that being a 'good Catholic wife and mother' simply meant that I was a baby machine. My church didn't care about me as a person . . . I was a woman . . . what rights did I have?"

Hopeless Choices

There was very little humor when Jake reflected on his experiences in parochial school. His Catholic heritage had left him both cringing and bristling. He was deeply angry that his childhood was so warped. He recalled the time when he was in church and the people were going up to the Communion rail row by row. "I sat there with little beads of sweat breaking out on my lip. I had a queasy feeling in the pit of my stomach. I had taken a sip of water that morning and Father George had told me that even a sip would mean that I had broken my fast. What was I going to do? If I didn't go to Communion, it would mean I had committed a mortal sin, and everyone would know. But if I did go, I knew that was a sacrilege and I really would be committing a mortal sin, and that meant straight to hell with me! So, there I sat, wondering which was worse, to endure the snickering and knowing glances of my classmates, or look into the fiery furnace of hell. I finally opted for hell and believe me, I stayed there for years of guilty shame and sick anxiety."

Many recovering Catholics have whole trunk loads of stories of the terrible things that happened to them. One man (a wonderful young father) sat in my office almost shaking with rage. He had recently found out that he had had a learning disability and was hyperactive in his earlier years. Even back then, he had known something was wrong with him, but at that time, no one knew that these were treatable disorders. "Almost every day, because I couldn't sit still, or didn't answer a question the right way, that nun would stick scotch tape over my mouth and make me sit in the waste basket . . . the dunce of the class. Of course, everyone in the room suddenly had oceans of waste paper they had to get rid of at once, so I sat there while they pelted me with paper balls . . . I don't know that I'll ever get over that feeling of shame and embarrassment."

There are countless stories about those big people in black, the stern, scowling priests, the ministers thundering hellfire and damnation, and the nuns rapping knuckles with steel-edged rulers, but not all the stories go way back in memory. Unlike the bitter woman who almost died in childbirth, some of the traumas are more recent.

Conscience Control by Others

Birth control had become such a major issue in many a marriage that the couples felt hopelessly trapped. Young families with not enough money or strength or even desire to have more children faced their priest's admonition to use the frequently unreliable rhythm system or the bleak alternative of abstinence, which, more often than not, caused dissension that truly weakened the bonds of the marriage.

Thousands and thousands of people were caught in this bind and finally resolved it for themselves, often contrary to what their church allowed. But they are furious that their religion pushed them into such a position of razor-edged guilt.

Others look back and recoil that at the tender age of seven years, the "age of reason" was reached. From that moment on the child was held accountable for committing mortal sin. As children, their heads were filled with stories of eternal hellfire. Fear became their main orientation toward God, the inflexible keeper of the rules.

However, the point of these pages is not to condemn religion. Right along with all the horror stories are the touching memories of millions, feeling the very breath of God flow over them as they knelt in a darkened church. And that breath was a delicious warm cloak warding off the cold. They tell of marvelous, empowering contact with a priest or nun who had an irreversible, positive influence on their lives. Many of us recall with sweet fondness the smell of the incense and a profound sense that "everything is all right" while participating in an ornate, mystical ritual full of Latin and pageantry.

Rather than condemning religion we need to take full responsibility as adults, that whether that experience with religion was positive or negative, black or white or any shade of gray in between, religion is not God. Regardless of what our past religious experiences may or may not have been, the quality of our walk with God is up to us. It is neither excusable or necessary to abandon that stroll with God in the cool of the evening because of religion.

Starting to Sort It All Out

After reaching a degree of maturity, some people are able to dismiss all this negativity as simply indicative of the times they were in. No one knew any better. Everyone was doing the best they could with what they had. They shrug it off and go on.

Others are filled with absolute rage. For them, it is inexcusable that they were taught that their religion was the perfect and indeed the only road to God. The church was the keeper of all truth about God. She (meaning "the church") and she alone was the only valid interpreter of God's will for them, having assumed the role as sole authority capable of deciding whether God was satisfied and pleased with them.

Today, the complaint many intelligent, responsible people have about religion is that it first attempted to make them into and then treated them as children. Children are those protected from responsibility because they are incapable of making the hard decisions or subsequently dealing with the consequences that such decisions create.

In the past (and in some pockets still today) the church's attitude was certainly patronizing. If those influenced by such an attitude have not been able to heal and move on, it is entirely possible that, again equating God with religion, they have chucked the whole sorry mess.

How clearly the signs of such influence remain even in those who have not walked away. A sure indication of such patterning is "doing it because I have to" as a child would, out of fear, with no sense of personal responsibility or of the emotional, individual commitment that adults make to anything meaningful to them.

Many others are simply sad. Saddened that at this time in the planet's history when there is such a need for spiritual content, for charismatic leadership and magnanimity of spirit, there seems to be such a vacuum in religious response. They are saddened that Sunday after Sunday, when the opportunity is so great to say something worthwhile, to get a shot in, the chance is missed. They love and care, and are loyal and ready to charge the gates of hell if someone will only raise a flag. They are saddened that all too often the bugler is mute or charging after minutia.

One can wonder how many filling the church pews on Sunday are there out of habit and routine—let alone fear—as opposed to an eager, enthusiastic involvement. "The best thing that could possibly happen to me," a very devout Catholic friend (who would never dream of missing Mass on Sunday) recently told me, "is a quick sermon, a short Mass, and out on the links by noon!"

Another very dear friend of mine, who had had no particular religious training, went along with me on a fishing trip many years ago. We were just outside a little town in Wisconsin and it happened to be a Sunday, so he agreed to come along with me to Mass.

Now this friend is a very spiritual man and certainly is not against religion, but he is not carrying around any extra baggage either. Well, we went to this service and not only was it boring, it was very bad liturgy. The old priest's sermon rambled on for twenty or thirty minutes of totally unrelated thoughts with no particular point whatsoever. It was just terrible. When we came out, my friend turned to me and said, "That was really awful. Why would anyone go to such a thing as that?" Of course, he didn't know all about hell, he didn't know that if you didn't go to Sunday Mass you were headed straight in that direction. He didn't know that when we were growing up, he was one of the "bad guys" and wasn't eligible even to date one of my sisters, or they would have been in deep trouble. He didn't know any of that. No, somehow he didn't know that because of the official stance at the time, since he wasn't a Catholic, he was, in the eyes of the church, the "bad guy"!

Whether the liturgy is capable of evoking a personal participation is a whole other question. It is important here to see how easily we either walk away in anger or remain with the mentality of a child while attempting to accomplish the most significant and adult feat of our lives: walking hand in hand with our friend, God.

This is not an effort to make an apologetic for the Catholic church. There are all kinds of recovering Catholics of whatever denomination, and what they are recovering from is very real. Real pain, real hurt, real issues. Real harm was done in many lives. Whether anyone else in your family or among your friends understands it or not, sympathizes or not, you know your feelings. You have a right to your feelings and truth as it is experienced by you.

Just Exactly Who Is a Recovering Catholic?

As we continue, it may be helpful to get a pencil and paper. Then, when we outline these different categories in more detail, make a few notes and see if you feel you fit into any of this.

Perhaps the phrase *recovering Catholic* is a misnomer for many and should be changed to *Catholics in need of recovery*. They are the ones who are simply stagnant in their hurt, anger, and rage, bristling with hostility, unable or unwilling to do anything about it. They certainly are not recovering from their negative religious experiences; they are not recovering Catholics but are Catholics (and all the others) who are in need of recovery.

How Can We Tell If Someone Is in Recovery?

A recovered Catholic would be someone who has worked through the issues of anger, fear, or despair and has found a contented, forgiving, and joyful spiritual life, either in the Catholic church, in another denomination, or simply in a rich, spiritual, personal inner life.

Who Is in Need of Recovery?

Let's outline some categories of Catholics who now find past religious experiences an obstacle to a loving walk with God.

1. First come those people who do not look back with huge amounts of anger and hostility but rather with a great deal of grief at all they feel was lost. This is typified by the woman who remarried but would still like to be active in the church. Such a person may desire to be on the Parish Council, or whatever the governing body for the particular denomination is called, or perhaps this person would love to teach a religion class. These are the folks who have excluded themselves from all religious practice because of a divorce, a second marriage, use of birth control, or because of an abortion in their life; and it makes them very sad. They want to be a part of the dance and feel banned from the dance floor.

2. The second category would be those who have remained in the church, who have no "legal" reason not to be there, but essentially, they have dropped out. And they are mad. They are disgusted that the rules have been changed. They want the Mass to be in Latin again. They are furious that all their lives they didn't eat meat on Fridays, and now they can't wait to tell you how they always hated fish. It seems they can recollect every single Friday that they were ever offered a hamburger but were forced to turn it down because they were afraid they were going to hell, and "nobody seems afraid of that anymore!" They are mad because now it is all so easy. A whole lifetime of sacrifices counts for nothing. They may not say much around the church, and they possibly still go to Mass, but they

ally dropped out of the life of the parish. Since these
we suggest they are many, are not going to participate in
aningful way, it is no wonder that some people say that or-
dina. y church parishes are rather boring, that it is hard to get any
action going, that not much ever goes on. If in fact there is a percentage of people sitting in the pews, week after week, who are
"dropouts" falling under this wide net of recovering Catholics who
have not healed old wounds, then obviously it is very hard indeed to
generate spirit among such hostile and unmotivated people. Whether
or not they were ever seeking spiritual growth, at the very least, they
have allowed the changes in their religion to become an obstacle to
their spiritual health.

3. A third category would be those people who are out of the church
and are furious. Many of these are persons in recovery programs of
some kind, perhaps for alcoholism or codependency or adult children of dysfunctional families. In the course of some self-help journey, they began to take a hard look at where all the shame-based
messages came from. Where did they get this great cloud of guilt and
hurt that seems constantly to hang over their heads? Perhaps in doing
Family of Origin work, they began to see how large their church
experiences loomed, and they realized as fact, that their religious
upbringing, which was supposed to bring them in contact with a
loving, saving God, instead increased their fear and anxiety, their
guilt and shame. In rage and disgust, they left. They left everything
but their fury. Frequently, this great insight as to the origin of their
pain, instead of helping, becomes a major sticking point, a stubborn
obstacle to growth. This is not to deny that that religious maltreat-
ment was real. These are the people we have described before, who
are surely victims of religious abuse. Understanding that is one
thing. Being able to pass beyond it is another. Might this be your
category? Out of the church but still furious . . . and possibly stuck
in that fury? All anger or resentment that we hang on to is going to
keep us resisting the peace of God.

4. A fourth and final category may include people who have left the
Catholic or any other church because of negative experiences and

have become part of another denomination. Some are most content and go on to real serenity. But quite a few, though they are practicing religious people, still experience difficulty because, like the napalm we mentioned earlier, the guilt and fear, shame, anger, and resentment still stick to them and continues to be the predominant imprint of their religious experience. Dealing with any religion becomes very difficult for them—a struggle rather than a homecoming.

In each of these cases we see how intellectually and emotionally God, religion, and spirituality have been lumped together so that it becomes difficult to achieve clarity in these very different questions.

Why Now?

Why do all these recovering people, Catholics and those from other denominations, seem so abundant these days? Why are there so many of them and where do they come from? First of all, nothing happens in a vacuum. Everything that happens is somehow related to something else. One of the great spiritual movements of our time started with Alcoholics Anonymous, which in turn led to the family program of Al-Anon, and then as a natural sequence, people began to realize how growing up in an alcoholic household had affected them. It was only another short step before people realized that it didn't have to be alcoholism, that any dysfunction would inevitably affect the children in the family. So kids growing up with a parent or parents who were workaholics, or who raged—silently or violently, or who were absent or cold or emotionally unavailable were equally bent out of shape. Therefore, huge numbers of groups known variously as Adult Children of Alcoholics or simply Adult Children of dysfunctional family systems have sprouted up.

Religion Loosens Its Grip

Another reason for the flocks of recovering Catholics and others is that for most people today, religion isn't as binding. There are probably as many people as before who still believe in hell, but they don't seem to be so perturbed about missing Mass on Sunday or not going to confession on Saturday, and Fridays are no longer required to be "fish or macaroni" days. In any event, there just doesn't seem to be the panic about falling into the fiery furnace. Today, people feel freer to reflect on their own religious reality, to question, to criticize, to think.

MANY PEOPLE ARE SEEKING HEALTH AND HAPPINESS

A third way to account for so much reflection on past religious experiences is the current emphasis on health and well-being, the holistic approach of body, mind, and spirit. Freedom from guilt and worry is a cornerstone of such an approach. Obviously, those snared in the ropes of religious guilt are going to have to free themselves if they expect to find wholeness. So there are all kinds of reasons that we find so many folks claiming to be "recovering Catholics" or trying to recover from any of the more damaging doctrines of other churches. What we need to do now is to try to untangle the knots and put ourselves on the road to genuine spiritual growth.

Where Do You Fit In?

Are you still practicing your religion, Catholic or otherwise? Or are you, whether religious or not, actively concerned with your own spiritual growth, content and happy in your relationship with God? If not, perhaps one of the four categories described earlier seems more to define your situation: grieving over the loss of your church life because of some rule you feel you have broken; attending church but, because of all its changes, sensing it simply isn't the church you grew up in any more; trying another denomination but finding it just doesn't seem like the "real" church; or experiencing such anger you don't want anything to do with God and a spiritual life.

Anyone of us who grew up in dysfunctional family systems learned to live forever coupled to shame. Our shame-based messages are not static, dead things. They are alive. They are the hinges our lives swing on. So much of what we do in recovery is to discover where those shamed-based messages come from. And we find that they come not only from the family we grew up in, our Family of Origin, but they also are frequently rooted in our religious background. Keep in mind that this is not just about and for recovering Catholics, but for anyone brought up in any religion that damages through shame. Catholics by no means have a corner on that market. Whenever we get some insight about the source of guilt or shame-based messages, we find, nine times out of ten, there was a religious orientation for it, and with the current emphasis on family systems, this orientation has come under intense scrutiny.

POINTS TO CONSIDER

Let's take these points into consideration. To begin with, rather than being terribly angry at religion about the damage done to us, I would like to suggest that the worst that was given to us through our religious training would probably have had little or no effect at all if the groundwork for it hadn't been laid in our Family of Origin.

Think about it. If we grew up in a family system where we learned that we were unique, lovable, special, neat, wonderful people, then all the hammering on us about being mortally sinful kids bound for hell would not have had nearly the impact that it did. Please note, when we were little, our parents were our first "God." If our home was one in which play was celebrated, having good times was important, self-worth was predicated just on the joyful fact that we existed, we had a solid base for a good self-image. Because we saw our parents as "God," we would have believed in ourselves and been able to carry this positive with us all of our life. All the churchly imperatives and "shoulds" we may have learned in religion, such as "idle hands are the devil's workshop," or "go collect money to ransom pagan babies" or stay busy, busy, busy or we'll be sure to get in trouble, and we all know where we go from there, would have held no terror for us. It is terribly important, in the context of recovery, not to single out one whipping boy, such as our religion, but to see it in the context of our whole life! The areas where we have the most to complain about in religion are the same areas we need to work on in our Family of Origin issues. So let's spread the blame around, if blame we must, and not let a resentment become an obsession, which, of course, then becomes an obstacle to real personal spiritual growth.

This is a good time to point out that all of this applies equally to those people in positions of authority in the church who did so much harm to us. We need to remember that many young women entered convents before they had time to know anything of the world. They knew nothing even about their own bodies, and no doubt had never even heard of P.M.S., and probably did much penance, puzzled as to why they had been so cross in class or harsh to a particular student. The thundering preachers or priests surely learned their hatchet theology at their parents' knees, never having dared to question its truth. Somewhere back there they were shaped by their family and religious background. Someone or something taught them to be who they were. We all are taught to be who we are. A particularly mean-spirited person was, without a doubt, a person who was damaged just as surely in the way we may have been. Hurt people hurt people. To make matters even worse, these poor folk felt they were commissioned, that it was indeed their duty to save our souls!

ONE WAY TO FIND OUT

A revealing exercise: Write down, as specifically as possible, the main areas of the complaints, resentments, or hostilities you have about your past religious experience. Do this in a column on one side of the page. Perhaps your list will include such things as "they taught me that I was a terrible person" or "they made me afraid of God" or "the church and religion were all about rules." On the other side of the page, check to see if these were not the very same principles you were taught at home in a more fundamental fashion by your Family of Origin. If one of your resentments toward the church is that it taught you to fear God, did you perhaps fear your father? Or was there fear of another authority figure in your home? If your complaint is that you were made to feel that you were a sinner, stupid, and inept, or that you never knew your catechism well enough to get the gold star pasted on your forehead, then let's look at how it was at home. Were you made to feel that you were clumsy, that you could never do anything right, perhaps that you didn't clean the kitchen well enough, cook the meal well enough, or your grades were never good enough? In fact, you were not good enough. You were basically inferior and inadequate in almost every way. It all fits together, doesn't it?

Perhaps as you grew up, religion just became a vast set of rules and laws that were impossible to keep, constantly leaving you with a sense of guilt and impending doom. Was the same thing true in your Family of Origin? Were there unreasonably high expectations so that no matter how well you performed, you always fell short of the mark? Did you grow up in a system of demands that were inflexible, heartless, void of any human warmth? If any of this is true, it leaves us vulnerable to the worst that is in our religious upbringing.

Recovery Is Recovery

Our attitudes may come from our homes and religions, but regardless of where obstacles come from, ultimately our quality of life is our responsibility.

Those people who can look back and laugh, who can play "Catholic Trivia" games with glee, or who enjoy a sort of Catholic can-you-top-this session, those people surely are the ones who grew up in homes where they never experienced that awful kind of damage.

Then there are those people who are eager for a spiritual life with God, but who feel that because they do not have the official sanction of the church owing to some religious technicality, they are somehow not worthy of God. And there are those whose experiences have left them so cynical and damaged that they have given up the journey entirely. Some just linger wistfully outside the church doors, and others stomp off empty-handed, vowing that they don't need anything or anyone, including God.

This book is dedicated to those people, whether in or out of the Catholic church or any other religion, who, when they found religion flawed and unacceptable, left it behind, but in so doing left God behind also. They have so confused God with church and religion, they have turned their backs on both.

It Just Won't Work

You may be saying to yourself right now: "It is easy for you to write about all this, but you don't know how much I was hurt by. . . ." And you are right. These thoughts are an intellectual overlay of some very emotional issues. But let us point out that indecision, resentment, anger, and perhaps a tiny dash of self-pity simply don't work. They simply do not make for a life worth living. You may have every reason in the world to stay angry, to stay excluded from any religion, to toss out the whole process of spiritual growth because your knuckles were rapped as a kid or some obscure, meaningless point of theology was crammed down your throat on a daily basis.

Who Loses?

Even worse things may have happened. Anyone so injured has the right to be angry forever. The trouble with that is, resentment victimizes the one who won't let go. You lose. You can't have a happy, contented, serene life and hang on to a hateful past. It just won't work. Reason it out. Reason isn't all bad in the context of emotional issues. Reason provides the basis for understanding, acceptance, for-giveness, letting go, moving on; those steps do work. Regardless of the overwhelming emotions involved in delving into one's past, we need to make real, hard decisions about the quality of our lives, the role we will allow past religious experiences to play.

A New Approach to Responsibility

In October, 1963, the Second Vatican Council met in Rome, ush-ering in momentous theological changes. Catholics were directed to something called the "internal forum," as opposed to the "external forum." Translated into very simple terms it means "grow up." When we operate on the internal forum, we take the responsibility for where we stand before God by the decisions that we make. Op-erating on the internal forum means that whether or not the official church says we are qualified to belong to the community of whatever and participate in the sacraments, we are the ones who make that decision. No longer do we give total power away to the pope, the priest, the nun, the church; we do not give that power to anyone and certainly not to ghosts from the past. We are to take the responsibility for defining who our God is. We take the responsibility for making the final decision about whether or not God is pleased with us. We do not ask that someone else give us permission to receive the sac-raments and be part of the church. We do not need someone else's permission or blessing to leave the Roman Catholic church and practice our religion in a different denomination, or as the case may be, in no denomination. We alone make those decisions.

EVERYTHING CHANGES

It becomes clear that when we start to grow up and make our own decisions about who God is, what God wants of us, what is pleasing to God, what is tolerable in our religious belief and what is not, then everything changes. God becomes infinitely more real than God could ever have been on some third grade level of faith when someone else told us who God was. When we decide that we are competent to know who God is to us, suddenly our spiritual life with God becomes personal. Only that which is personal can be real for us.

Will It Really Make a Difference?

What difference would operating on the internal forum make in your life? Let's look at a possible scenario. Perhaps you are in a second marriage, and although you would like very much still to be active in the Catholic church and receive Communion, your theology tells you that this second marriage is against the rules. Quite possibly you went to see a number of priests who told you that not only would they not officiate at your wedding ceremony but that in fact if you went ahead with the marriage, you would be entering into mortal sin, and with a fair degree of icy disapproval, they reminded you that that meant you would be going to hell. In fairness it must be noted that there are many priests who, with compassion and charity, would counsel the path of the internal forum.

Relationships, like people, can die. For many reasons, perhaps, that first marriage of yours simply died. Possibly it was never alive in the first place. Perhaps your spouse or you, or both of you were chemically dependent. Perhaps marrying each other was not a healthy, holy, mature decision to make in the first place. It may never have occurred to either of you to seek an annulment, which would declare that there had never been a valid marriage at all. So you didn't do that, and the marriage died.

Now comes the moment when you have to confront God as you know God to be in your heart. You know you are not going to live the rest of your life as a celibate, single and alone. As sure as heaven is within, you know that to try would be to do great spiritual harm to yourself. But if you remarry the church will say it is a mortal sin, and that puts you in a terrible box. You know you cannot or should not live as a hermit, but if you don't, then there is another sin, and hell is just around the corner. Somehow, in your heart of hearts, you know that is not what God as you understand God to be wants of you.

Perhaps you meet someone and find that you both are healthier, more grown up, definitely not kids any more. And you fall in love. Your lives are infinitely enhanced by knowing each other. Rather than trying to live some kind of unnatural life without any emotional, physical, or spiritual contact with another human being, you hear God saying, "Be together, love each other, treasure each other, and find me in that love!"

You go ahead and get married. Of course, it can't be in the church, it can't be blessed, and you are definitely not going to get any pats on the head.

Then comes that longing to be part of the sacramental system again. Can you partake of the bread of the Gospels?

The question is, who is going to deny you Communion when you walk up that aisle? Chances are the parish you belong to is so large that the person giving out the Eucharist is a layperson and wouldn't have any idea who you are anyway. That person doesn't care about what is going on in your life, so what is apt to happen? No sign is going to drop down over your head that says "This person is in mortal sin and must be denied the Host." Of course not. Operating on the internal forum, we are the ones who make the decision whether or not to go to Mass, whether or not to receive Communion, not based on someone else's theology, not based on fear, not based on somebody telling us that God is mad at us. Our decision is based in our faith that "I will take the responsibility, and I will take the consequences. I will decide for myself."

God Wants Us Free

Soon we will come to see that everything we know of God tells us that God wants us to be free. God wants us to be healthy, whole, free, loving people. We need to become grownups and make our own decisions about the will of God for us on a day-to-day basis.

This theme has been around for a long time in our literature. The chapter entitled "The Grand Inquisitor" in Fyodor Dostoyevski's great novel *The Brothers Karamazov* illustrates it most powerfully. Dostoyevski had no great love of the church, but he had a great love of God. He describes how Christ returned to life and was immediately thrown into jail. The night before Christ's execution, the Grand Inquisitor came to the prison to plead and bargain and to question this Christ who had been taken captive. He knew that Christ was God. And he knew that he was going to kill him. The incredible dialogue goes something like this. The Grand Inquisitor says to Christ, "You don't love the people. You are telling the people to grow up. You are telling the people to make their own decisions. You are telling the people that God wants them free."

The Grand Inquisitor's point is that people don't want to be free. They want to be told who God is and what sin is and whether or not their souls will be saved. So the Grand Inquisitor says to Christ, "You put an intolerable burden on the people when you tell them to grow up, to make their own decisions, to find God as they understand God to be. People just don't want that."

Of course, Christ's answer was then, and I believe is now, "But the people need to grow up. The only way people ever find a real and loving God is when they grow up and make the decision in favor of God themselves."

Once we have reached the point where we understand that it is vital to make our own decisions, it can no longer be valid for free adult people to say, "I quit" because some priest back in 1953 stood us up in front of a class and humiliated us because we couldn't name all the holy days of obligation. That is quite simply a delusional rationale for refusing to grow.

A Jesuit theologian, John Courtney Murray, basically wrote the "Doctrine on Religious Freedom" as propounded at the Vatican Council. In this document, Murray outlines the sanctity of each individual person's conscience, the decision-making ability. He makes the point that the first decision of conscience is not simply to decide, but to study, to read, and to think. What is the truth? We need to consult with wise people, to dialogue with others, and after we have prayed, thought, and studied, we no longer make decisions just because they feel good to us. We are trying to find the truth so that we can operate in favor of the truth. We pray. We open up channels to God so God can send us light and humility and strength. Light to show us the way to truth. Humility so that we can get our "wants" out of the way. And finally, the strength to live the truth.

In this light then, acting on our truth might very well be going to the Eucharist instead of staying away. This is not, however, a license to do any old thing we want. Quite the opposite. Operating on the internal forum is learning to take responsibility for our own truth as we see truth to be, and that comes as the direct result of serious, intense study, long discussion, and heartfelt prayer.

In subsequent chapters we will examine the spiritual steps that lead us on the road to simple maturity. We will need to be willing to listen to the external forum, but also to be very willing to operate on the internal forum. God speaks to our hearts every day. We need to take down the barriers, to listen to God whenever God speaks to us. The God who loves us speaks to us. What is God saying to us? No, not ten years ago or thirty years ago. What is God saying to us today?

There is a beautiful poem by Edna St. Vincent Millay that seems to illustrate the point. The name of the poem is "Renascence" or "rebirth." It is a very long poem where she describes the process of becoming fed up with life and wanting to die. Her character in the poem wished it so much that she did die. And for a while, the peace and quiet and darkness of the grave was comforting to her. But slowly, she began to miss the sight of trees and the sound of birds. She began to miss being alive! So she wished to be alive again, and she wished it so much that she was granted life again. In this great poetic reality, this renaissance, there is a short section of the poem that speaks eloquently to the real hope for these pages. It goes like this:

> About the trees my arms I wound.
> Like one gone mad, I hugged the ground.
> I raised my quivering arms on high
> And I laughed and laughed to the sky.
> Until at my throat a strangling sob caught fiercely

And a great heart throb sent instant tears into my eyes.
Oh, God, I cried.
No dark disguise can ever hereafter hide from me
Thy radiant identity.
You cannot move across the grass
But my quick eyes will see you pass.
Nor speak however silently
But my hushed voice will answer thee.
I know the path that tells thy way
Through the cool eve of every day.
God, I can push the grass apart
And lay my finger on Thy heart.

How wondrously said! May this book help guide you who are frozen, who have denied yourselves the pursuit of God, and yet may once have seen the face of God in a religious experience. My deepest, most heartfelt hope is that I can reach those of you who are in this dilemma, to tell you that you do have options. God is far deeper and wider than religion. Just because you have made a choice about your religion, and even that may change as attitudes and perspectives change in the future, you do not have to abandon your search for God. This truly is up to you! Real recovery frees you up for your spiritual journey.

May you lay your finger on God's heart, never again to have God walk by and be missed by you because you are so helplessly fixated on the past that you miss the passing of freedom.

I Wanna Go Home

If, on giant wings, we encircled our planet
coming to rest upon, within, the hearts of our fellow
pilgrims,
listening with tender compassionate ears,
seeing with the eyes of poets,
feeling with the hands of a gentle carpenter caressing his
wood,
what we would be touching more than any other river of
emotion or longing,
would be a desire for home.
Whatever home is.

2

Who God Is Not

The term *recovering Catholic*, as we said, is a wide net indeed. Included are those who may have wrenched themselves out of the church in rage, those who have separated with deep regret, and those who sit bitter and smoldering in the pews each Sunday.

For some, the answer to this prickly dilemma concerning their religion, as we have already pointed out, is to be found along the path of the internal forum. Invoking this path for many, of course, requires more than simply deciding to do it. To walk the path of internal forum requires a rather highly developed sense of self-actualization. Those who desperately need the approval of others find this way difficult indeed.

The point is, however, that wherever people may find themselves in this broad mix, or whatever problems they may have in first owning and then correcting whatever damage was done at hearth or altar, the opportunity to walk with our God is always there. The opportunity as well as the responsibility. We have all been affected by our past. None of us need be victims of that past.

God, Religion, and Theology—All Different Realities

As mentioned before, a major confusion leading to tragic conclusions is our tendency to equate God, religion, and spirituality. No matter how much this impression was pounded into our heads, verbally or non-verbally, by teachers who may have scared us to death—it just ain't so. If we are to do ourselves the favor of embarking on a deeper, closer walk in the cool of the evening with our God, we must learn to distinguish between God, religion, and spirituality. In that distinction our options and opportunities are made manifest.

I have found this diagram helpful in making this hugely important point leading us to a greater spiritual freedom:

Us . . .
in need of
Grace

The three lines shielding us from God's gifts are Negative Religious Experiences, Cruel Theology, and Religious Communities That Do Not Live Up to Their Names. The purpose of the illustration is obviously (I hope) to show how they can become stubborn obstacles cutting off the warming light of God's grace. "Can become" does not mean "must remain."

As we investigate these particular realities through understanding and a willingness to take personal responsibility for our journey, we can transmute opaque to transparent. We can turn walls into windows, steel into glass. It is a terrible thing to think about God standing outside knocking, loaded down with gifts, and finding no one willing to open the door.

Let us consider these realities in turn:

GOD

No concept, theology, or word about God is wide enough to explain God. God cannot be put into a box. God resists any and all efforts to limit what God can or cannot do by constantly demonstrating (often in the most incredible ways) that God is bigger than we are!

As sure as some human builds a corral of some sort to contain God, in an instant God is outside running over some distant hill. It was for this reason the ancient Jew was forbidden even to have a name for God. To name a thing, in that culture, was to have an inner knowledge of—and thus some control over—what was named. But God was the forever unknowable, the forever beyond whatever the religious Jew could imagine. So that they would be reminded of that fact, God had no name.

This is not to say that nothing can be known about God (for this reason, faith tells us that God loved Jesus into existence, precisely so we would know something of God). Not all concepts, words, or theology about God are idolatrous or unimportant. Far from it.

No human being will ever know the full meaning of love either, but that doesn't stop poets and philosophers from endlessly writing about it. And each time genuine words of love are said and people of love pass through the shadow of our lives, we are enriched. We may not know the totality of love, but we certainly know more of its nature and power.

So it is with God. And all that God means. And all that God does. We could see the magic God has in store for us, the show put on for us daily, if only we would pay the price of admission.

The homily (sermon) I heard last week was about the perception that God is much more a verb than a noun. The priest did a marvelous job of urging us to think of God as an active agent in our lives, with us as is our heart beat, our thoughts and breath, rather than as some static object like a tree that just stands there.

No one can reveal God to us as God is. No more than anyone can tell us exactly how we feel or respond to some event in our lives, or the unique special way we perceive our reality or love those whom we love. Such realities are far too personal for anyone to have full knowledge of, let alone be able to tell us what they should be. How would they know what they "should be"?

Such is God the verb.

No one but God knows what God has cooked up for us. No one but God and we, walking in the cool of the evening, know what passes between us. Only we know our special jokes and the special words all friends and lovers share. Who could ever possibly tell us what these are supposed to be?

I am a recent, first-time grandfather. Incredible how such a tiny piece of humanity can orchestrate so many other lives. The faces! Oh, it is that magical splendor in all the faces gazing upon that tiny person and those irresistible fingers and toes. What does love mean? Who can ever completely capture its depth? The look on the face of the young father when he came out of the delivery room must have been much like the countenance of Moses coming off the holy mountain after talking with God. All the mother could say in those relaxed moments after the delivery was, "He is so beautiful! So beautiful!"

Only she has any real idea of what that means. So it is with God. God is revealed to each of us in ways so personal and special that not even the most insightful and famous of theologians could begin to touch.

We dare not throw this wonder away in the name of resentment. Any such resentment toward past religious experience is petty in comparison to what we discard when, because of it, we abandon openness to God. Whatever God's gift of special meaning may be for us, it is our unique responsibility to go forth and find it. Over and above the help anyone else can give us through advice and spiritual counsel, our search for God is totally other than that. It is beyond that. Just as no one can tell us who our God is, neither can anyone take God away from us except by our permission.

Most everyone reading these pages knows any number of facts about God or names for God. What they mean to us is a totally different matter; what they mean to us is up to us. We know, for example, that Jesus has been called "the lamb of God who died for our sins."

Only by deep personal reflection and investigation could that sentence have any real meaning for us. What might our sins be that have so distanced us from the light of self-esteem and respect? How have they felt? What have they cost us? What have we done to ourselves—and others?

We know this lamb of God, in some mysterious way beyond our fathoming, died for us that we might be saved. Have we felt saved—rescued? Have we allowed ourselves to experience redemption? Do we know the liberating sensation of moving from darkness to light?

If we have had that singular experience then no amount of dreary, dehumanizing experiences can possibly tarnish the power and grandeur of God in our lives. We would not, could not, allow even such debasing incidences to matter.

RELIGION

To go on with our exercises, under the topic "Religion," write down some of the main experiences with your religion that you perceive to have become obstacles in your relationship with, or experience of, a loving God. You may want to refer to the first chapter where we outlined some possibilities. Perhaps for you it was the enormous stress caused by the emphasis on sin. Was your struggle with what is known as scrupulosity, that no matter what you did (or do) it was somehow sinful and you knew God was going to get you because you never did anything right? Or perhaps it was a shaming, degrading, or embarrassing experience with one of those awesome figures of authority, the preacher or the priest, the nun or the Sunday School teacher?

Whatever they may be, write down several of those religious recollections you may have, and then look at them very consciously. Understand that *God is not religion*. God is other than religion. If one of your memories involves doing the Stations of the Cross every Friday during Lent, and for you, that was a profoundly negative experience, remember, that is *not God*. If you remember being told that dancing was a sin, which meant you missed all the proms during high school and were always looked down on as going to that peculiar church, that was *not God*. God is not religion!

THEOLOGY

Now on your paper, write down "Theology." *God is not theology about God.* This is a major block for many people. Theorizing about how many angels could dance on the head of a pin, or that eating meat on Friday was a mortal sin, or that you were going to hell for receiving Communion after you had had a sip of water, all of that is *theology about God*—that is *not God.* We have so clumped God in with all those speculations and rules that when they became ridiculous or cruel, we turned our backs on them. All too often, however, we also turned our backs on God. Discarding terrible or stupid theology is surely a very good thing, but discarding God because we have mixed God up with that theology is a tragedy.

A sad example of this comes from a dear little lady who was recovering from multiple dysfunctions in her life, one of which was religion and her anger toward God. A grotesque memory from her childhood was of a grandmother who used to make her kneel in a bathtub full of marbles to pray the rosary. It didn't take this woman very long after she had grown up to see that this was monstrous. But what she hadn't done was separate her grandmother's rather twisted theology from God. God didn't ask that child to kneel painfully on glass marbles in a bathtub and pray her rosary in order somehow to give God honor and glory. That strange notion came straight from the convoluted, torturous theology of her grandmother. Accepting that was the next step this dear soul had to take in order to discover her God, loving and kind, who never would have asked such a thing of a little girl. When she did, she was set free. *Theology is not God.*

Still under the column "Theology" write down some of your basic theology about God: what you were taught and what you might answer if asked questions about God. Then, go to your internal forum and ask yourself, "Do I really believe that? Does that make any sense to me?"

The story of my father, who for a large part of his life had an antipathy toward the Catholic church, may help to illustrate this idea. We never talked about his feelings, but I always presumed that they indicated some heavy-duty antagonism toward God. However, they came from the theology in which he was raised. It seems that when my grandfather (his father), whom my father most dearly loved, fell in love with my grandmother (his mother), a staunch Irish Catholic, Grandfather was not a member of the church. In order to be married in the church, indeed in this case to be married at all, Grandfather had to become a Catholic. So he asked what it took to become a Catholic and was told that he had to be baptized. Well, he didn't believe in it, but if having some priest pour a little water on his head was what it took to get his bride, then that is what he determined to do. He did and they got married in the church. But he never went back. He never believed. He lived his whole life without being part of the church. In those days, faith was not seen by the church as an interior ascent to the truths of God.

Since my grandfather died before I was born, I have no idea if he was spiritual or not. That is not the point. When it came time to die and he had not darkened the doors of the parish church since his wedding, his Catholic children, especially my aunt, were coming around begging him to let them call a priest. "You are a baptized Catholic, Dad, and if you don't reconcile yourself through penance and absolution, you will go to hell." His comment then, way ahead of his time, was "Why would I want a priest now that I am dying when I never wanted one while I was living? I didn't believe then and I don't believe now, and I refuse to be a hypocrite." So, my grandfather died "outside the church." Because of the prevailing theology at the time, my dad probably believed all of his life that his beloved father had been condemned and put into hell by the church.

It is a very heavy burden to carry a resentment toward God because of the theology of the times, a theology that puts God into that little box that is not God. God is wider than theology about God.

Perhaps you have lumped God, religion, and theology all together and have thrown it all away because at one time the church was so strict about not eating meat on Friday. Then, seemingly arbitrarily, it changed the rules; so someone you know ate meat on Friday and went to hell, but now anyone can go out and eat a big steak on Friday and it's okay. Ridiculous, you say, and toss it all out. Think about it. Think about becoming mature in your faith and the internal forum, taking responsibility for who you are.

Theology and the Internal Forum

God is wider and other than theology about God. Taking the time now to do some thinking and writing about God will begin to reveal your personal theology about God. What does God want of you? Regardless of the past, the strict nuns who perhaps humiliated you, the scary or boring Sunday School lessons, regardless of whether you never did or always had to get gold stars plastered on your forehead for memorizing the Baltimore Catechism or the names of every book of the Old Testament, what is your theology now?

Recall now the conditions proposed by John Courtney Murray who wrote the great article on freedom of religion and conscience. He said, "Our first duty in conscience is to educate ourselves." Once you have discovered what your theology currently is, what you truly believe, ask yourself if you have considered studying it. Are you searching out wise people to discuss it with, people who really have something to offer? Internal forum is taking responsibility for your own theology. Who is God to you? What does God want of you? What is sin? When are you in the wrong? How do you reconcile yourself to God, to yourself, and to the human community? You see, there really are all manner of theological questions that have an effect on you daily. Your answers will dictate how you live your life. Remember those lines drawn in front of the sun that blocked the life-giving rays? When those three elements have really been thought out, the lines aren't obstacles any more but magnifying glasses that focus the love of God into real power in your life. What is your theology?

Religious Community

The next element we need to examine is church community. For you, this may have been a parochial school; it may have been, or perhaps presently is, your parish church or congregation. Could you be one of the many who've said, "I've quit going to church any more because it is full of hypocrisy." When asked, "What do you mean by hypocrisy?" there follows a long complaint such as "I mean all that piety and moral superiority is left behind when people come out of the church and practically run you over in the parking lot. And those pompous ushers, the pillars of the church . . . everyone knows half of them were out getting drunk Saturday night and there they are, all pious and proper on Sunday morning telling you where you can or can't sit. I'm just sick and tired of it. They are all hypocrites." Next ensues a general deploring of the infighting, quibbling, quarreling, and downright fractiousness of these supposedly religious people. What's the surprise? They are fallible human beings bringing with them all the methods of coping, good and bad, that they learned growing up.

God is other than the religious community. He is other than the people you like or don't like and with whom you worship and go to church. Clearly, there is a touch of hypocrisy in stating that anyone who is flawed or fallible or a sinner is a hypocrite. With that statement, all human beings qualify as hypocrites, including the person making the statement.

If there is anything at all meaningful in our particular religious community, if we get something from it, then why not get involved ourselves? Get on the committees or councils or vestries and influence things our way. Take an active role. They won't let us, or they won't want us, we say? Who is "they"? Going to our internal forum, we soon find that "they" are the decisions we make in our own heads, probably projections of our own wounded selves from our Family of Origin! Yes, it is true, religious communities sometimes are not a very clear mirror of the face of a loving God. But God is more than religious community.

A favorite story of mine concerns an Al-Anon group at a church where I was stationed. Our Al-Anon group was forever borrowing the big coffee pots of the Ladies Guild. Sure enough, one Monday morning not only was the cord to the coffee pot missing but there was a sign attached to the urn announcing that this pot belonged to the Ladies Guild and was not to be used by Al-Anon! About as unloving and petty as a church group can be! It could have ended in uproar. It would have been quite natural for the Al-Anon folks, some of whom were members of the parish, to say "Well, if this is religion and this is God, I quit!" And indeed that had happened. But when the group looked at the other side of the story and listed the good points, such as being allowed to use the building, paying no rent, having an enthusiastic supporter in the priest in charge who was an excellent preacher and who promoted Al-Anon and Twelve-Step programs, well, so what if they had to bring their own coffee pots? Suddenly, the issue wasn't all black and white. They didn't have to respond with childish, self-defeating attitudes that equate God with any church community, theology, or people who were and always will be blemished. They didn't have to proceed angrily to abandon God because of flawed humanity, thus bringing their own spiritual growth to an abrupt halt. Who is God to you?

Allow me to wind up this section with a parable from Scripture. Now even if you are of the variety of recovering Catholic who is so turned off at the mere mention of Scripture or the Bible that you want to throw this book across the room—don't. Rise above it and read on. We have to understand some things if we are going to find the truth.

As a practicing Roman Catholic priest, I was going through some very difficult turning points in my life. The lovely parable of the Lost Sheep became an important beacon for me through that time of deeply troubled waters. I used this Scripture in a meditative manner. It went something like this: If you recall, the setting is that Jesus is speaking of the love of the Father. Out of a large flock of one hundred sheep, one strays away. The shepherd becomes so concerned that even one of his sheep is lost that he leaves the ninety-nine to find that lost one. Unbeknownst to the shepherd, the little stray had not only wandered off but had also fallen over a cliff, gotten itself tangled up in a thorn bush, and couldn't get free. To make things even worse, it was hanging in the branches only by its hooves and soon would surely fall many miles down to its death. Meanwhile, the shepherd struggled on, searching for the sheep. At last, he found the frightened little beast, and when he did, he didn't slap it, or mock it, or get angry with it. He didn't shout or abuse the animal in any way. Instead, he carefully and lovingly lifted the terrified sheep and, putting it on his shoulders, returned with it to the flock.

Who is God? Not just religion, not just religious experience with a flawed religious community, and not just theology about God. Who is God to you? The fact is, we cannot run farther than God can reach. God is always seeking our return. God is always seeking our comfort, our health, our safety, our freedom. There can be no Easter without Good Friday, but God is always there to help us pass from death to life if we will but allow it. *Who is God to you?*

Religion, Theology, and Community

What is religion actually? Religion is humankind's best effort to focus the persona, the power, and the message of God in an understandable and effective manner for the human race. Religion is humanity's best effort to make God known and present among us, among Adam's race. Please note the two parts of that: (1) "Man's" and (2) best effort. Looking at religion, we are looking at "man's" best effort. (The masculine form is used because, from the beginning, men have been in control of the laws, direction, and nature of the church—and obviously not always for the best!)

What Do We Mean by Man's?

Man's means "of man." Religion is of man, of humankind. This does not preclude the idea that parts of the church may very well be of divine origin, may be of God. It may very well be that much of what we know as religion is directed by God, inspired by God, intended by God. But the fact remains that much of what is religion and religious is of man. That being so, why should religion then be any different than any other thing that man gets his hands into—defective and imperfect, at times downright ridiculous, not to mention unfair? Now why is it that we would expect religion to be any different? If it is of man, it is flawed, period. Yet we somehow expect it to be otherwise. Some folks say it is understandable from any other institution, but we were told that this was different. We were not only told but we were taught in school, we were brainwashed that this was different. We were told that it was of God. That it was perfect. At least we were meant to believe that it was perfect, that it was eternal, it was immutable, it was infallible. We were required to believe that "The Church" was other than human. Yet we cannot escape the fact that the church is peopled by flawed human beings. How then did we come to believe that somehow the church was peopled by perfect people who were holier and much better than we were?

WHERE DID THESE BELIEFS COME FROM?

We were taught to believe these things. We were taught that the professional religious people, ministers, pastors and preachers, priests and nuns and monks, because of their life-style, because of their spiritual training, by reason of their rather mysterious lives and their high calling, knew much more about God than we did. Obviously, they had the inside track to God. They knew what they were talking about, and if that were so, and they then told us that religion was God, who were we to argue or disagree? So, of course, we bought this line of reasoning hook, line, and sinker. Even when their all too real flaws showed up, rarely were they held to any accountability. Their loss of temper or impatience, even their alcoholism was to be ignored because we obviously didn't have the intelligence or the right to understand what it was all about. We were the ones who just didn't get it. With the lack of belief on our part that we knew more about our God and who God was to us than anyone else, and with no accountability on their part, naturally we totally swallowed the whole myth. Docilely (at least outwardly), we accepted the position that they were the sole arbiters and voice of God in our lives.

With the appearance of clay feet, disillusion sets in, causing more often than not, chaos and confusion. Again the flag goes up—it is time to grow up, to take charge of our own lives. Those huge, mysterious people, mostly arrayed in black, who solemnly told us the "truth about God," were and are just people. People like us. People who came to the seminaries and convents and monasteries for all sorts of reasons, some much more noble than others.

HOMES LIKE OURS

Like us, many of them came from their own dysfunctional homes, their own dysfunctional family systems, and like us they perpetuated and projected that dysfunction, their own preconceived ideas and understanding of God, onto God and religion. They too had Adult Children issues, issues around being accepted, important, belonging, having all the answers. They brought their baggage of Family of Origin issues, issues of security, the need to please, boundary issues around joy and play. Remember all the panicky trauma around the understanding and beliefs about pleasure! God only knows what their issues around pleasure were!

THAT SYSTEM IS GONE

They committed to a system that no longer exists, rooted in a spirituality born in Medieval Europe, a spirituality that, for example, saw the Black Plague as God's revenge for sin. A spirituality that through centuries of tradition reinforced some nasty character defects in the candidates, and made it desperately difficult for anyone to enter any kind of recovery, let alone challenge the rules handed to them. They were absolutely buried under the weight of time, never to be questioned. For some, this rigid system rolled off their backs—

for others, it stuck like glue. As for understanding religion—who were the religious people who taught us?

Indeed, those religious people who taught us and gave us our religious experience telling us what God meant, may very well have been touched by an element of Divine Gift in the form of vocation to religious life. But Divine Gift or not, those people who answered the call were and still are ordinary human beings with strengths and weaknesses, character defects and fallibilities, people who are sinful and always will be. It could be no other way.

A Look at Best Effort

Man's best effort. Let's get it really clear—best effort does not mean perfect. Obviously, man's best effort doesn't mean immutable, and it doesn't mean unchangeable. There have been such dramatic changes in religion over the past thirty years that one can no longer doubt that religion can and does change. But best effort doesn't always mean the best. All it means is that at the time, with the particular people involved, it was the best they could do.

We are capable of reaching into our past and bringing up on our mental screen a picture of that certain priest, nun, preacher, or teacher in our church or classroom. Our emotions can be felt now just as they were then. With great clarity, we truly see and understand who these people were—that their best effort to make the voice of God clear to his people came from fallible human beings. It still does. What they did and possibly now do may be wrong, it may be a mistake, it may be founded on faulty theology. Or it may just be the expression of imperfect, flawed Adult Children, acting out a need for power or control. Whatever the reason, it is, right now, the best effort these people can make.

Understand that living in the internal forum mode, our task is to grow up, comprehend, reflect on, and make our decisions about how much power we choose to give to those faulty, probably well-intentioned, perhaps quite intelligent and holy people . . . basically faulty and flawed people just like us, doing the best they can with what they have. No longer must we give them all our power. Humbly listen, yes. Blindly, unquestioningly follow, no. It is all a matter of spirituality.

WHAT DOES SPIRITUAL MEAN?

In a subsequent chapter, we will explore more deeply what we mean by the term *spirituality* especially in its position vis-à-vis religion. But for the sake of clarity here we'll define spirituality as the basic assumptions with which we interpret and deal with our lives. It is about who we are in relationship to the important issues of our lives, not only about our relationship with God. It comes from inside of us, and in that sense, everything we do is spiritual, from what we are going to have for dinner (are we treating our bodies with sacred concern?), to our decisions about our job, or a casual conversation with an acquaintance. Everything we do will somehow reflect what we believe, what our basic assumptions are about life. So when we arrive at a point of taking more direct responsibility for our religion with God, we have some serious self-examination to do. In order to grow, we must know and acknowledge our basic beliefs.

WHAT THEN IS THE ROLE OF RELIGION?

If the role of religion is to make the face of God clear to us in our time, then it should function in three ways. It should provide the seeker with (1) education, (2) rituals in which the mysteries of God can be experienced and shared, and (3) a believing faith community wherein the process and journey toward God is deepened, made possible and loving.

Education, ritual, community: how does religion do these three things? One way—and this is guaranteed—is imperfectly. At times, it does them badly. At times, it may seem that the church we go to has the most boring, uninspired, unspiritual liturgy or services imaginable. There may in fact be no real Christian community, just lots of people crowded into the church together every week to get through the Mass or worship as quickly as they can. Again, we see that it is simply man's best effort at this time.

Our responsibility is to grow up and accept the reality as it actually is. We find religion flawed, but could it be any other way? Would it be different if we were running the show? We think not. Once more, when we find it imperfect, we need to make some decisions about how much power we are going to give to this institution. How much are we going to allow it to become an obstacle on our way to finding God? How do we choose to expend our energy?

If all your old tapes are telling you that you do not have a right to seek your own truth, that you have no right to say no to something that makes absolutely no sense to you, that you have no right to question or criticize or to go your own way, then what? The only answer to that, and I say this from my heart to your heart with love and understanding and compassion, the only answer there is, is to become an adult! To grow up! Then, as with any other old neurotic rule you got from your past, make some choices. Take responsibility for your choices. Refuse to give up your intelligence and your power. It is your right and your responsibility to make your own decisions about your disposition with God. It is your responsibility not to give that power totally away to anyone or any institution. And that is the crux of the matter. You may or may not have the blessing or approval of your particular church representative or official. But do you have *your* blessing, do you have *your* approval? Who is it that ultimately stands before our God, both today and on that day when we pass through death? Who will be there with us to hear the words of light and life? I suspect that we are going to be there alone. No pope, no bishop, no minister, no preacher, no nun, no Sunday School teacher. Just us. Possibly the question we will need to be prepared to answer will be, "Did you do the best you could with the light you were given?"

Cutting Those Old Ties

In my counseling office, working with recovering Catholics, it is at this point I often hear a huge sigh of relief. It is frequently accompanied by an almost humorous shaking of the head, as if to say, "Well, I'll be darned, this is no big deal after all." And in some sense that is right. It is especially true if the sticking point is around some dumb chestnut from forty years ago. With a sort of controlled explosion, I have heard, "You know, I never believed that stuff about plenary indulgences in the first place." Right. (By the way, these days you might have a hard time finding anyone who has the remotest idea of what plenary indulgences could possibly be). Or, "I never believed I would go to hell if I didn't go to church on Sunday or if I ate meat on Friday." Right. Or, "I never believed masturbation was a mortal sin . . . or that dancing was of the devil . . . or that nine first Fridays was going to guarantee me a place in heaven forever." Or . . . here insert all the individual stories we have recounted that are negative experiences from third-grade mentality religion. Right!

That was then. Now is now. If there are some people who get a great deal of comfort in rituals such as nine first Fridays or praying the rosary or kissing the toes of statues of saints, fine. God bless them. Good for them. But it doesn't have to have anything to do with us as the individuals we are. Our lives are ours. No one else is responsible for them or will ever care as much about the amount of joy and serenity that we can achieve in our lives as we do. So why allow anyone else to diminish the quality of our spirituality and most especially if it somehow centers around some beliefs or rituals that to a large extent no longer even exist?

The Four Marks of the Church

Here is one interesting thought relative to the Catholic religion, and we ask the recovering Roman Catholics especially to consider this one. Please write down on the paper you are working with the four marks of the church. Remember, the four marks of the one true church with which we were so thoroughly schooled? They were that the church was (1) one, (2) holy, (3) catholic, and (4) apostolic. *One* meaning that all its members professed the same faith in Christ under one visible head, the Pope. *Holy* meaning that it was founded by an all-holy Jesus, that it taught holy doctrines and provided means of holiness to others. *Catholic* meaning universal, that it was the same everywhere, destined to last for all time, never failing to fulfill the divine commandment to teach all nations the truth. It meant that whether you were in China, Africa, or Hollywood, it was always the same. You could expect the same doctrine, rituals, and language (Latin), and you would be pretty much at home in any Catholic church anywhere in the world. (Obviously, this is not the case today.) *Apostolic* meaning that it was founded upon the apostles, by Jesus, and ever since then, every bishop has had the succession straight from St. Peter, who is considered to be the first Pope, and that has continued into the present. That was the really heavy gun, because it proved that we were the *real* church and the Protestants weren't, because the Protestants did not have apostolic succession reaching all the way back to St. Peter. (The Episcopal church claims this same apostolic succession.) Whatever truth there may be in each of these, it must be noted that they aren't the only marks.

Four Other Marks of the Church

There are another four. Based on the fact that at least part of the church is human, and therefore made up of fallible human beings, then these next four marks are equally true. The church is (1) sinful; (2) fallible; (3) changeable; and very definitely, (4) unfinished. It can be no other way.

The church is *sinful* because it is made up of flawed, sinful people as all of us are. So of course, we will find within the church, gossip. We will find hypocrisy. We will find every character defect known to humankind played out within the councils and guilds and clergy as well as the laity. We will find power plays and all manner of politics. The church is sinful.

The church is *fallible*. It makes mistakes. It makes mistakes in its decisions. It makes mistakes in its structures. It makes mistakes by refusing to grow and change when change seems so necessary and obvious to us. The church is going to make mistakes. Being made up of humans, certainly being intrinsically at least partly human, how could it be otherwise? The church is fallible.

The church is *changeable*. No one need belabor that point today as it is so apparent. A very few fundamental principles may not change, such as the divinity of Jesus Christ, Son of God who rose from the dead. But in every other respect, heaven knows that the church is changeable. Just that one item of eating meat on Fridays— probably even the pope and the priest do that now. Latin is out; women distribute communion and may one day even be priests. There well may be married priests. Almost everything of the church is changeable.

That the church is *unfinished* goes without question. The church is growing. The church is doing the best it can in its slow, ponderous, fallible way to adjust to the times. It certainly isn't finished yet. Revelation perhaps is finished if that is a point of any importance to anybody anymore. But the way we understand that revelation, the way we act out the revelation with our very best insights in today's world, changes all the time. The church is most certainly unfinished.

Other Denominations Are Going Through the Same Things

We could simply use slightly different language to apply all of the things we have been saying about the Roman Catholic church to any of the major denominations today. Changes and arguments about those changes rage throughout Protestantism and Judaism. Accusations about perverting the faith come from both liberal and conservative sides of the fence, from Catholics, Protestants, and Jews. Yet things somehow lumber on with fallible human beings trying to steer the course first this way and then that way. Those four other marks, sinful, fallible, changeable, and unfinished, apply just as thoroughly here.

Should We Just Throw Out All Religion?

Having said all of this, are we to draw the conclusion that religion is of no value at all? Does religion cause so much harm and damage that it should be avoided at all costs? Not at all!

Once we develop a mature, responsible attitude about our need to seek and find God as God would speak to our hearts, then religion, in its proper perspective, plays an important, helpful and to some degree, necessary role in leading us toward a full spiritual life. Once we stop demanding that religion be the final authority about us and God or demanding that religious folk be perfect, then we can be on the way to a new relationship with religion that can be infinitely more of God than anything we have ever known before. It is important that we recognize that. Understand that. Reflect on that. Church is about church community. Community is about people. We need other people.

I frequently hear people say, "Why go to church? I can find God while I am just sitting under a tree or up on a mountain top." Of course you can. But finding God in church or on a mountain top is not an either/or situation. More often than not it is a matter of both or neither.

Being critters of flesh and blood, we need others to celebrate our meanings with us if they are to be properly celebrated. That is why Christ said, "Do this in memory of me." That is why the Eucharist was left in the form of a meal, a meal to be shared with others.

Spirituality, if it is to be healthy, needs to be of the nature of a shared walk. To be sure, if all there is, is sharing with others, the journey becomes a shallow exercise in meaningless commotion. Healthy spirituality demands that a portion of the walk be of the hermit. We need to be quiet so that we come to understand and treasure the sound of our own voice. If walking with God is mostly a matter of being led by God, then we need to be silent enough to hear where we are being told to go. Prayer is more a matter of listening than talking.

But all that wisdom gained in the desert needs to be shared lest it become no more than idle talking to ourselves, which is dangerous as well as lonely. One's own self talk always makes sense no matter how insane it may be.

The fullness of all true celebration of what matters most to us is carried out in the flux of the journey within (the hermit) and the journey without (the poet sharing his vision).

This is the real problem with just abandoning a faith community. Where will we then share what is beautiful to us? Where will we find the support to continue our journey? Where will we be inspired by the marvels told by other travelers?

Communities that are worthy of the name are not a group of bored, impotent people gathered together in the name of routine or fear. They are those who gather around a central meaning to celebrate its vibrance in their lives and in that celebration ever to deepen its power.

Christian community gathers around the meaning of "God-with-us." Community that counts is generated by people who have already experienced that revelation in their lives (who God is to them) and who gather with other like-minded people to see what miracles have happened to them. Faith is not a blind intellectual assent to some dead dogma. Faith, like God, is a vibrant verb that shakes the soul like a dog with a fresh bone in its teeth.

God can, by all means, eloquently and exquisitely be found on a mountain top or in the strains of beautiful music. God should be found in any and all beauty. But if that revelation is not then shared in some ritual, some liturgy, the chain reaction stops. The meaning then withers or runs the danger of grotesque mutation.

The fact remains, we need one another. As powerful as the reflection of God is in our own lives, every other person also becomes a mirror portraying a wonder of God we would never have guessed.

On fantasy's wings I have often dropped in on the camp fire of the apostles as they went about their urgent business of opening the minds and souls of others to this new vision of the beauty of God. Can't you just see them, lightning in their eyes, retelling their stories . . . "You think that's something! Listen to this. . ."

We need each other's stories, the witness to God the verb, if we are to continue firmly along the path.

If none of this happens in your church community—find one where it does. Let us not cut off the bird's wings and then ridicule it for not flying.

When we reflect that the church was and still is fallible, when we recall or observe that both church structure and church institution may be riddled with frustrating, galling, appalling, power hungry political people, why be stopped by that? Religious practice and ritual change is not only to be expected, but should also be celebrated because at the very least it is an effort to make up for past faults and to focus the face of God as clearly as possible in this present time. The church is human. Religion is human. At least the part that drives us nuts is human. It simply is man's best effort. No more. No less.

Let us illustrate the thought of how true this is, dealing mainly with ritual. Remember earlier we explained that a main function of religion is to make religious ritual, which stands for a spiritual reality, become present for people. Recovering Roman Catholics are really going to relate to this because they have been so thoroughly immersed in rituals all their religious life. They will be entirely familiar with holy water and incense and probably remember when that little white wafer stuck to the roofs of their mouths. Heaven forbid that they ever poke a finger into their mouth and try to unstick it. That was strictly *verboten!* Do we really think God would have sent us to hell for touching the Host with our finger? Or was it, then as now, people just doing the best they could with the light they had?

Rituals and Symbols

Many recovering Catholics have long since rejected some of those rituals and religious symbols as meaningless, boring, or silly. Of course, any ritual or symbol is only as important to us as the meaning behind it—in other words, what it really symbolizes to us. Think about it. Rituals are powerless when either the participants in the ritual have never experienced what the ritual is meant to convey, or when that ritual and the symbol it uses no longer convey the experience for which they stand.

First we have the experience. Rituals are created to keep the experience alive. Then symbols are fashioned to be used in the rituals. The accompanying chart should make this clearer.

SYMBOL

EXPERIENCE 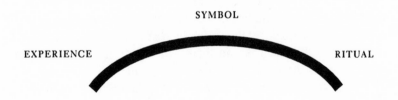 RITUAL

We see how the line between *experience* and *ritual* is topped by the word *symbol*. We have an experience that is ritualized through symbol, which expresses the meaning and deepens the experience. In this way, experience, ritual, and symbol are related to each other.

To clarify further, let's look at some real-life examples. There is no way to make a ritual meaningful and important to us if we have never had the experience, or if it is unrelated to anything we have stored in our own minds. Those of you who are familiar with the Twelve-Step programs, specifically Alcoholics Anonymous, know that the goal of the program is sobriety. Sobriety is celebrated with a lovely little ritual where people can commemorate thirty days of sobriety, sixty days, three months, nine months, one year, and on up to twenty and thirty or more years. During the celebration, the so-called birthday person receives a medallion that states the number of months or years of recovery. Usually this person's sponsor, the person who has held the alcoholic's hand, who has cajoled and badgered, who has shared joys and tears, ups and downs, who has hung on the phone, sometimes in the middle of the night, proudly hands the medallion to their "sponsee" and thus shares in the accomplishment. Attending one of these "birthday" celebrations, one would be hard-pressed to call it boring or meaningless.

Now look back at our chart: experience, ritual, symbol. Here people are sharing the experience of the struggle for sobriety, sharing the experience and the feeling. What an accomplishment those first few months are, what a sense of peace comes with those years piling up! The experience can be felt all over the room.

The ritual is the little ceremony, the handing out of the medallion, the sponsor recounting something of the struggle and character of the person who has now achieved whatever amount of time of recovery. Frequently, the recipient passes the medallion around the room so that each person there can hold it a minute and rub personal good thoughts, love, and courage into the coin.

The symbol is the medallion, and quite probably millions of these are carried around in people's pockets or worn around their necks to remind them of the quest they are on and to celebrate it when they look at the medallion, to reflect on it, to keep them mindful of the mission, to keep them safe. The experience, the ritual, the symbol: They are all enormously meaningful and clear as long as the experience is there and the ritual expresses the experience.

In this day, the experience of Vietnam remains very clear to millions of us. Countless young men and women were there. Equally affected and involved were their wives, husbands, daughters, sons, sisters, brothers, mothers, fathers, indeed all their families and friends. An enormous symbol of that whole experience exists, and it is quite simply named "The Wall." If you have not been there in person, no doubt you have seen it on television. The Wall is a symbol of that whole war. And countless rituals are carried out in relation to The Wall as relatives and friends, comrades in arms, and even strangers are confronted by it. Letters are left, flowers and flags are stuck in the ground, people stand before it, eyes closed, talking or praying or running their hands over a name again and again, somehow telling their loved ones who never came back things they wished they could have told them. These rituals are not meaningless! They are not boring! Because the experience is real, the symbol is full of power.

A different example of the same idea would be a wedding. Two people have traveled through the process of learning about each other, have experienced a courtship, and have now decided to live a life of committed love. They ritualize that through some kind of wedding ceremony. The ritual is there in order to express an inner meaning. The symbol most frequently used is a wedding ring, although there may be many others. Here we see the experience is love, the wedding ceremony is the ritual, the ring is the symbol.

Think on this aspect of ritual and symbol as well—symbols take on the meaning with which we invest them. There are those who find Christmas, for example, the worst time of the year, finding no comfort in the symbolized spirit of the season represented by Santa Claus. Who in the world would not love Santa? Someone who has been terribly hurt during the Christmas celebration.

Symbols are just symbols. They mean what we bring to them.

Thanksgiving for many is a time of gratitude and a celebration of plenty. At root it is a celebration of survival during a long, cold winter. Thanksgiving symbols abound from pilgrim dress to roasted turkey. Who doesn't love that? Probably many Native Americans. The symbol of plenty for the Europeans and their descendants was a symbol of the beginning of the end for those here first.

The point is, once we have invested a symbol with meaning that is both personal and powerful, no one can ever take it from us. It is safe within us.

Recently the Catholic church (and many of the other eucharistically centered churches) has made enormous efforts to change the way it ritualizes many of its sacraments. There is a real effort to fit the ritual to the meaning, to fit the experience behind it. Once we have opened our hearts, opened our minds to push the grass aside to try to find our own God in our own world, we can bring personal meaning to the ritual. We can infuse those religious symbols with our own meanings. No one else knows what any particular symbol means to us because we have brought our own special meanings to the ritual ourselves, and that makes the ritual and the symbol uniquely ours. They are ours in a way that no one can take from us.

What Do We Lose When We Leave the Church?

If we have not been able to accept the responsibility for our own decisions—the internal forum—and we have decided that we simply cannot forgive the past, we stand to lose a community where we can share and symbolize our pain, our recovery, and our own very real resurrection. Perhaps we have not even tried to seek out another parish or denomination. Sadly, we may miss the joy of learning, of deepening our spiritual quest in the company of others on a similar path. But the deepest loss we can sustain is the loss of our journey with God. As we have seen so graphically, when we throw out one dimension of our spiritual life, all too often that means we throw it all out, excluding God from our lives—the very heart of the matter.

If we are honestly convinced that we have made a well thought out, reasoned, healed decision to leave the church, and it feels right, so be it. But if we have not made all those efforts that lead to health and wholeness, perhaps we might want to consider that we need to do a little more work.

We all know about Easter. Easter is that radiant time when we celebrate the fact that Christ rose from the dead. Death to life. No one knows more about this than a person recovering from holding onto a lifetime of resentment, a person who has experienced some great peace and freedom from letting the past die. People come to me all the time who have done just that. Inch by inch they have worked their way through some enormous anger or resentment and have felt it lifted from their shoulders as if it had weighed twenty tons, and now they are wonderfully, miraculously free. Death to life.

I have seen many people who were in bondage to a chemical dependency, alcohol or other drugs, and certainly they know all about death and failure, the promises to quit, then using or drinking again, hating to get up in the morning only to look in the mirror at the misery and shame reflected there. And then the way out is found. Suddenly this person's head is held high, the reflection in the mirror brings a smile. The image is that of a face one can like. Death to life. Any recovering person knows what that means, knows it in a way that is infinitely personal and real. When that meaning is ritualized or the experience is poured into the ritual of the church, it becomes heart-meltingly meaningful.

So now what does the experience of Easter mean to this person? Well, we can always say that it is just a bunch of meaningless objects, such as candles and incense and sprinkling of water, because we haven't brought any personal meaning to it. But when we imbue it with our own recovery, our own death to life experience, we find God and the ritual comes to life, it is real, it is ours. We belong. We are home.

There Is More

A *ship of fools? Noah's ark? Paradise lost?*
The rich and the poor, illiterate and brilliant—
from behind monastery and convent walls as well as the
          glare of disco and cat house,
the universal hymn rises,
I wanna go home, home to something more—
a more not counted or possessed,
not collected or stolen,
a more of the spirit that touches deeply,
that wipes away tears and brings joy to fulfillment,
a more that fills the quiet empty spaces with rainbows
          rather than fearful beasts.
There is more. We know that.

3

Codependency: The Walk with God

Q uestion: What place has codependency in a book about recovering Catholics?

Answer: These pages are not just about recovering
Catholics but about the more fundamental issue of how to achieve
a healthier spirituality—how to undertake a joyous, lifelong walk
with one's God in the cool of the evening. Obviously, negative religious experiences can be and are an obstacle to a serene, faith-filled
journey. Wipe the fog from the mirror of a debilitating, God-
obstructing religious problem and most often you will be looking
straight into the ugly face of codependency. The distress expressed in
the inability to achieve a richer sojourn with God is usually inflamed
codependency acting out in a religious setting.

One recent client, for example, was a man carrying a terrible
chip on his shoulder. Half growling, he muttered darkly, "Don't
even know why I'm here. I gave up on religion and God a long time
ago. They both lie." A married man, he had contracted a sexually
transmitted disease long before AIDS had made its appearance. Guilt
filled his heart. No doubt with a certain amount of sincerity, he had
promised God he'd be good if only his marriage could be saved. "Not
six months later," he spit out with fierce justification, "what do you
think happened! I got the damn disease again. Lies," he thundered,
"all lies. They taught me God never lets you down, and now look
here, I end up laid low again."

Somehow the concept of personal responsibility had never pen-
etrated his blindness. He never did figure out that it wasn't God who
was cheating on his wife, nor was he being abducted by sex-starved

females! His problem was not with religion, but with irresponsible, destructive habits underlying his perception of what religion and God's role were all about in the first place.

Another example that comes to mind is the man who, when he drank got drunk, when he got drunk got mean, when he got mean he took it out on his wife and children. One day, he showed up at church after a stint in jail for drunkenly kicking in his own front door and assaulting his wife. On this fine morning, he stood in the back of the church as Moses had stood before the Red Sea, arms raised high in a prophet-like stance, proclaiming: "I am here to do thy will, oh Lord!" When I asked him what in the world he was talking about, the concept of sobriety or ceasing to bang his wife around were not part of his plan. Rather he was rambling on about founding a new church that would lead millions to the light!

Underneath the religious life we are living, or the religious life we may have abandoned, is the person who is living it. The more that person is spiritually disfigured with any of the many masks of codependency, the less the religious situation is a cause of the loss of God, but is rather more a symptom.

Remember the story about the Al-Anon group, the Ladies Guild, and the coffee pot? With a finger snap everyone in that group could have stormed out of the church never to return, lumping God right in there with the small-minded, mean mentality that would deny the sharing of a coffee pot. More than most, however, Al-Anon members are well aware of the foibles of their fellow human beings. To their everlasting credit, these church-mouse-poor but stalwart folks figured, "people are people," snuck in a hot plate, and heated up their Sanka until their kitty allowed them to get their own coffee pot.

Underlying most of what is negative in religion is codependency.

Codependency Defined

As popular as the term *codependency* may be, there still are many for whom it is unfamiliar—and many more to whom it is familiar but still quite baffling. What exactly does this mysterious, overworked, and often misused word mean? Originally the term denoted the often dysfunctional behavior of the spouse of an alcoholic, but gradually it has broadened and become all-encompassing, covering the many, varied, and all-too-obvious dysfunctions involved in human living.

Space and the purpose of these pages prevent any detailed analysis of the history, cause, or remedy of codependency. Other works have done that, including my books *Stage II Recovery* and *Stage II Relationships*. For our purpose however, allow me to offer this basic explanation for the way the term will be used throughout the following chapters.

Codependency and its allied terms (Adult Children syndrome, dysfunctional families, shame, inner child, and so on) indicate various disfigurements along the normal path to maturity, resulting in the formation of painful, habitual patterns of thought and behavior that reach out from the past and affect how we live our lives today.

For example, people who were repeatedly taught as children that their thoughts and feelings were unimportant, years later may still experience anxiety when called upon to express an opinion. That is certainly codependency.

Someone else may have been traumatized early on by another's anger and perhaps never learned the difference between anger and rage. For them, all anger is rage. Their response, learned early and deeply, may be to avoid any and all conflict whatever the cost. It is conflict that generates anger and for them, anger means to be victimized by rage and that is to be avoided no matter how much self-esteem is sacrificed. Though this negative learning may be decades old, such people frequently experience terrible tension whenever strife seems imminent. They run from conflict like a scalded dog. That is codependency.

Others may simply have learned that the only way to get what they want is to act the bully. For them getting their own way, intimidating and forcing their views and opinions on others is as natural as breathing. Due to whatever mixture of nature and nurture, they quickly learned that the way to get the bright red truck in the sandbox was simply to walk over and take it. They greedily snatch up those red trucks in exactly the same manner today. Codependency.

Common to most forms of codependency is the basic belief that because of some innate fault and flaw in themselves, love will always be a stranger at their table. For reasons many such afflicted people cannot quite put their finger on, they are sure they do not deserve to be loved or that love simply will not be their lot in life. They are convinced no one could ever *really* love them. Whenever a relationship begins to generate any amount of true intimacy (with all the terrifying vulnerability intimacy always demands), anxiety crackles like too much electricity in a high-tension wire. Often the anxiety causes the individual to figure out some way to diminish the intimacy, although such closeness is his or her heart's fondest desire. All such intimacy and relational issues are codependency issues.

Clearly these become serious obstacles to a healthy spirituality. Those issues always express themselves in that complex community interaction we call religious or parish life. It is that same flawed community life that many recovering Catholics (or Catholics in need of recovery) find so offensive that they leave. And all too often, once they have departed from religion, they feel they must also stand God up on God's offer for a date in the garden.

There is nothing magical or even especially bizarre about the concept of codependency. In fact, nothing is more rock-bottom common sense. It is not particularly insightful to grasp that a child who was severely traumatized in some manner by fire may well show signs of overreaction to something as commonplace as a blaze in the fireplace. Others may find it wonderfully cozy and safe, but for the person who was hurt thirty or forty years earlier, it is quite another story. While some cavort gleefully around a roaring bonfire, and others find the dying coals blissfully mesmerizing, this poor oddball, fire-scarred codependent hangs back, finding flames or embers anything but soothing, exciting, or fun.

Once the reasons and patterns are recognized, of course, such behavior is not really strange at all. Once the codependent fixation is understood, it all makes sense. But when the affected persons do not see the pattern, they feel terribly strange, perhaps inadequate, like misfits. Thus the vicious circle of self-defeating action and re-action revolves one more time.

Certainly with enough desire and effort, the codependent person can learn to recognize and overcome these fears and obsessions. No one need be victim to the past, no matter how ruthless a master it may be. Once the connection between early imprinting and the present seemingly eccentric behavior is seen and understood, there will be less guilt, less beating up of oneself wondering, "How could I be doing this?" or "Why do I keep doing the same old thing—I must be insane." Not at all. The more clearly past patterns are seen, the more obvious the expressions of those patterns become in today's perceptions and actions.

The popularity, energy, and power of all the contemporary self-help and codependent literature is that it helps explain all of those baffling, irritating present-day bumps in the road. Bumps that seem such a waste. Bumps that add up to pure absurdity. Bumps turned into thick mud on the window of God's love trying to penetrate our souls. In the light of codependent technology, the puppet wires become visible, and therefore can be cut. Any youth who has ever run through a backyard at night fleeing some adolescent prank knows full well how important it is to locate the metal clotheslines that used to stretch across many a yard! If nothing else, to know when to duck!

To reiterate, a person's problems with religion, and for many, the far more important question, their relationship with God, may go way beyond just a negative religious experience. A deeper, extremely potent underlying issue might well be a little understood or recognized case of codependency. Indeed, it may be so poorly understood as to be invisible, leaving the person in the same precarious position as the youngsters running through their neighbor's dark backyard. If they hit a wire they soon figure out what nearly decap-itated them! But in the case of undetected codependency, often the individual just lies there with a nearly broken neck never realizing what happened or why!

Call and Response

It is sound theology to understand the entire panorama of "God-with-us" in the context of call and response.

Some eighteen hundred years before Christ, a man known to us as Abraham lived in a place called the Ur of Chaldees. God had a plan for him as God does for each of us. Through all the cultural milieu and the personal strengths and weaknesses of this man, God called. God invited Abraham to leave his land, possessions, and gods, to come apart, to become the father of a great nation dedicated to and centered around the worship of God, the one true God who now spoke to Abraham.

The theological term for this call is *election*. Abraham was the child of election.

He responded. Not without doubt and with no small amount of dancing sideways as well as straight ahead—but still—he went. Thus the chosen people were born. Hundreds of years later, Moses received his call. From the famous burning bush, he was called to leave the desert, march into the court of the most powerful king of the time and demand freedom for a bunch of unimportant slaves who were captives right along with a great many others. No simple task. He was asked, as his spiritual ancestor Abraham had been be-fore him, to let go, to believe there was a power greater than him at work, to obey its calling and get going.

Moses too responded. Not perfectly. No human being ever does. But he picked up his staff and headed for Egypt, eventually to lead a band of terrified people on a long torturous journey, marching them out of slavery to freedom.

God called. That call was, as are all God's calls, an invitation to do what for us alone would be impossible. All that is required for those who are the children of election is to hear and make a best effort stab at response.

The theological term for this committed response is *disciple-ship*. After Moses, twelve hundred or so years passed before a man known to us as John the Baptizer responded to the call of his God. John was asked to confront the powerful local King Herod and by the quality of his own life make straight the road upon which Christ the Redeemer would come upon the human stage.

Come he did. Christ's life was one long call or invitation to those of us who came after to answer this call. The call to disciple-ship was a call to think with a new mind, to see with eyes not of this world. It was a radical call to overcome the blindness and hardness of heart that tempts us all. Don't be fooled by show, Christ said. Who is justified before the Father. . .? And he told the parable of the poor widow quietly dropping her last coin into the metal collection pot right after the rich man had made a big, noisy show of depositing his pocket change. Be my disciple, follow me, don't be fooled . . . see to the core.

Stop being judgmental, he said. Who is better than his neighbor? And he reached out to a frightened, embattled woman taken in adultery, flying in the face of all the "better" folk who would condemn her. See with your heart, he said. Put down the stones. There is no place for brutality and cruel killing of one another. Reach out the hand of welcome rather than the fist of condemnation. Follow. Follow me.

Be done with self-pity, he taught. There is always a road home. There is always a way to find forgiveness. And he told the parable of the Prodigal Son who sank about as low as any human being could. But this son decided he had had enough of living in darkness. He rose up and thought perhaps his father would take him back as a servant if not as a son.

Yet calling out as clearly as a cock at dawn, Christ said the father rushed out to meet his son, placed a ring on his finger and a cloak over his shoulders, and threw a huge homecoming party. The father cared not one whit what the son had done. All that mattered was that the son who was dead had come back to life.

Christ calls. We respond. Perhaps feebly, but what counts is that at least we respond in the best way we can at the moment. And here precisely is the dilemma. What exactly is it that blocks our response? A major obstacle is the resident codependency clogging the arteries of our spiritual hearts.

Six Conditions of Discipleship

For the sake of illustration allow me to suggest six qualities or conditions necessary if we are to respond to the call of election by which God invites us to each new day. Hopefully, it will then become very clear how codependency is actually the opposite of these conditions. Recovery from codependency is absolutely essential if we are to incorporate these conditions and skills into our lives, necessary in order to respond to God.

TRUST

The ability to trust is a prime directive of discipleship. The whole idea of "God-with-us" is that we are safe in believing that we are not alone. The main thrust of the Christ event is that we are justified in believing that no matter what may come our way, we do not have to deal with it solo.

Trust, of course, goes far beyond an answer in times of trouble. Those of us who are able to live in the sunshine of trust have the sense of an abiding presence that enhances our every hour. This trust is the ultimate answer to soul crushing loneliness.

An exercise often used in trust-building events, whether on a religious retreat or in enhancing camaraderie in an office setting, is to ask participants, facing away from the group, simply to fall backward—trusting that the others will catch them.

Such is the constant state of security of one who can and does truly trust in the Lord. Life deals us all blows that knock us backward. The question is, is anyone there to catch us lest we fall? Trust says yes!

CODEPENDENCY REPLIES

Those damaged by negative imprinting universally express difficulty in trusting. Of course, this is to be expected. All codependency is about learning that life is not safe, that what should be there is usually not there at all. Codependency is about the touch that was never given in gentleness, the denied kiss. Locked in that emotional position, that belief system of abandonment, the individual has, at best, a limited ability to respond to Christ's call to trust totally and to let go of false anchors.

Lacking trust, all codependents have a devil of a time with commitment. Commitment always entails vulnerability. Only a fool would become vulnerable when there is a conviction that disaster is just around the corner.

The tragedy here is that one of the sweetest of all human experiences is the sense of well-being resulting from knowing with a knowledge far beyond mere intellect that "it is safe to be here." It is finally gaining the ability to trust that has healed many a heart broken by the sledgehammer blows that crushed their ability to trust in the first place. Healing comes inch by inch until at last some glorious conversion experience of belief chases the night from the heart, enabling the person first to doubt, then wonder, then dare to believe, then finally gladly shout—I know you are there for me! I can count on you!

Regardless of how many church services a person may attend or, conversely, how passionately religion has been discarded, the fact clearly remains that if that person is unable to trust, he or she will never find the way to a rendezvous with God.

SURRENDER

Surrender, as used in this context, is far removed from "giving up." It is the opposite of retreat. Instead, surrender in a healthy sense is the ability, based on maturity, to give up the need to try to control outcomes over which we have no control in the first place. Surrender is the coming to grips with life as it is, knowing there are some things we can change and others we cannot. And as the famous "Serenity Prayer" advises, we had best know the difference.

The constant plea of Christ is that we surrender, not as fallen victims subject to the whim of the victor, but rather that we surrender to that loving walk, that manner of being in the world that would strew flowers rather than devastation as we pass.

The sole condition for keeping God's company in the cool of the evening is that we "till the garden." The Hebrew word used here was *obed*, a word meaning obedience. Obedience is the ticket to paradise.

Rather than a servile situation, this kind of obedience is in our own best interest, the manner and method of operation that truly promotes our happiness and the well-being of the human community. To surrender to our need for honesty, integrity, community, and the pursuit of beauty is simply how human beings work best. Each and every time we go against the grain, disaster follows. Abuse of another not only damages the victim but also victimizes the abuser.

CODEPENDENCY REPLIES

Codependents are notorious for the need to control. Surrender cannot coexist with codependency. When we have learned not to trust, and become hardened into the belief system that it is all up to us, to count on no one but ourselves, then of course the need to take full responsibility for all that is around us is an absolute necessity. For this reason codependents are furious worriers. With so much out of our control, yet feeling responsible for everyone's well-being, what else is there to do but worry ourselves sick?

An oft quoted axiom in the Twelve-Step programs is "Let go and let God." A favorite twist on that is "Let God or be God." Those of us unable to surrender are incapable of "letting God" and end up condemned to the constant attempt to be God. Tough duty!

Many a sermon has admonished, "If you pray, why worry? And if you worry, why pray?" On the surface it makes great sense. The flaw is that it presupposes that the individual is *able* to surrender, *able* to trust. With the ability to trust a choice truly exists. Without that ability, choice is not possible. If underlying and undetected codependency makes this choice an impossibility, then such admonitions simply drive the individual into greater shame or loss of belief that he or she have a right to "be here with all these worthy people." Try as they might, they simply cannot "live up to" such common-sense spiritual advice. *Want to* doesn't always mean *able to*.

More than a few recovering Catholics have left their religion precisely because they felt they couldn't live up to what was being asked of them, such as trusting or stopping the worry. Not knowing any better, it seemed to them that they did have a real choice and that they had deliberately chosen the less spiritual path, when actually, for them there well may have been no choice at all.

ACCEPTANCE

The greatest torment of one who loves is not the loss of a beloved partner but to love one who cannot or will not accept that love. Jesus was seen sitting upon a hill overlooking Jerusalem and weeping. No matter how he loved them, they would not love in return. Though he would "gather them as a hen gathers her chicks under her wing . . . they would not." Destruction was soon to follow. This destruction was not punishment from a vengeful and repulsed lover. In rejecting the love of Christ they also rejected the walk, the way of life, the intimate bonding that joined those who gathered close to the flame who is God. Rejecting the surrender to that way of living, they would choose a path of selfish blindness. They would refuse to look out for one another and thus in innumerable ways they would all die for lack of caring.

The central issue of Christianity is not that we love Christ, but that we accept that we are loved by him. The critical point here hangs on the hinge of acceptance. If we can accept that we are the people of election by God's own wish and design, then there is no need (nor are we able) to earn that privileged status.

It is ours because it was given to us. Our task is not to knock ourselves out trying to be perfect (impossible) but to relax, accept the gift as given us and enjoy the ride.

With humble acceptance we are released from the need for perfection and the crushing fear of not measuring up. With the acceptance of acceptance and the subsequent laying down of all those responsibilities, we can take our place in the garden with heads held high and songs in our hearts.

When this acceptance isn't present however, there are no limits to the ugliness of the monsters—frequently in the name of God. A choice example of someone leaving religion, church, and everything to do with God was the woman whose devout grandmother made her pray the rosary while kneeling on glass marbles in a bathtub as punishment for her sins.

It is impossible to earn the love of God. It is impossible to make up for our flaws, failings, or downright sins. The reason for this is because it has already been accomplished. It is already done! We are loved because God has decided to love us.

We are redeemed because Christ has chosen to lift the latch barring us from hearth and home. The gift is at the door. It is a perfect gift. It is all that is needed. The task is to quit going into contortions trying to manipulate favor. The task is simply to open the door and accept the wonderment of it all.

CODEPENDENCY REPLIES

Smack into the wall again! No matter how many times we may read or hear those concepts of love, no matter how desperately we *want* to clutch that gift to our very souls, if we are basically, fundamentally unable to accept acceptance, then it is simply a no go. *Want to* is not necessarily *able to*.

By its very definition, and all that it implies, codependency would prohibit those who were brought up in prolonged dysfunctional situations, who learned that they were basically flawed and undeserving of the better things of life, from ascending to the freedom of surrender and acceptance.

Codependents' lives have been filled with punishment, to a greater or lesser degree, beset with accusations such as "putting on airs" or "pretending to be more than you are" or the order "you made your bed, now lie in it!" Countless times when they got up enough courage to reach out for the gentle, safe embrace of a loved one or the encouragement and approval that people who love one another always bestow—they were given not a kiss but a stone.

Each time this happened, slowly, like concrete setting, their inner vision of themselves and the world began to form and harden. They became what they had learned. That learned lesson of inadequacy and distrust makes it impossible to accept the invitation of God.

Codependents find it next to impossible to believe that they are loved. They suffer from a potent, high-level fear of abandonment. The normal need we all have for intimacy and love becomes, in their cases, a desperate drive since it has been so achingly, devastatingly denied them. Unable to accept that they are lovable, they go about the business of finding love in the only way possible for them: either they run from the pain or they try to earn love. No matter how much they do, or is done for them, no matter how much they give, or is given to them, no matter how hard they try to feel worthy, or others try finally to break down their wall and scream into their souls, *"I love you just because I do, not for what you have or what you do for me but just because you are you,"* it is all in vain.

That is the tragedy. It matters little whether it is another person or God who loves them; the barrier simply cannot be broken. For them the walk in the garden is a forced march, stemming from that awful sense of responsibility and the great fear that they will ultimately be told to go back home. For them there is no gentle, warm, caring—to say nothing of fun—stroll in the garden with their friend God because they cannot conceive that God would ever even want to be in their company.

Puts one in mind of the man weeping on that hill outside of the city.

VISION

In the darkest of worlds, Christ was the brightest of sunshine. He was the golden light on top of the mountain. He was the joy in the midst of doom. Everything about Christ spoke of hope—the best is yet to come, and that time is now!

Christ's resounding proclamation was that the *Kingdom of God is at hand*. Not just what may happen to us after we die, but *now*, for the Kingdom is within. Even a superficial reading of the parables and miracles of Jesus speaks to the finding of beauty and meaning right here and right now. The Kingdom is a way of life, a way of seeing and understanding the world we live in, which in the ways of the human heart has not changed in two thousand years.

We who seek the Kingdom first will be spared the frustration and disappointment of filling barns and attics with treasures only to find that they are worth nothing. Seek the Kingdom and in that community of believers, we will find love aplenty. We will find honesty, support, patience, and wisdom in those who walk the path of justice and mercy.

Dare! That is what Jesus was talking about. Dare to believe, to fling our aspirations skyward, to rise above small-minded earthbound thinking and dare to be free. Dare to be great. Dare to risk thinking that each one of us is truly a child of God with all the power and privilege that implies. You belong, he kept saying, you belong so stop worrying about it and start living it.

While I was working in a very deprived inner-city parish, an occasion arose when I was to take our boys' eighth-grade basketball team to an all white, middle-class banquet. The boys were not at all sure about leaving their neighborhood. They neither trusted those who would be in attendance nor believed that they would not be deliberately embarrassed in some manner. The time came for the awards to be given out and one of our boys was named to come forward and receive his trophy. Fear sat on his heart like a ten-ton elephant, almost paralyzing him. Sensing the young man's terror and comprehending the reason behind it, the guest of honor, a tall, handsome, famous African-American professional player stepped down from the dais, strode to the boy's side and said, "Don't be afraid son, come with me. We'll go up together."

"And boy," he said, "you hold your head up high."

A precious moment if ever there was one. A million times a million times that scene is repeated in our lives. Christ is here. Always the same message, ". . . we'll go up together . . . hold your head up high." It's here. It's all here.

The question now is one of trust, acceptance, surrender, and believing the vision that indeed—yes—we are called to come up and receive the prize!

CODEPENDENCY REPLIES

Enter the villain. Puppies don't have to be paper swatted too many times before they learn to stop leaping into the air and jumping on people. They soon get the drift that there must be something wrong in trying to get higher than they are.

Inherently, codependents have learned to be grateful for crumbs. Their expectations have been so blunted by those paper swats that they are afraid to dare for anything much beyond survival. Perhaps for them it was the emotional unavailability of parents or constant sibling rivalry where they always came off second-best to the resident family hero, or maybe they were always expected to know but were never given the time to learn.

Whatever it was, they deeply internalized the lesson. Stay on the ground, keep out of the way, be a chicken not an eagle, and never, never hope for too much.

Reaction to this lesson may have resulted in becoming an over-achiever, eternally trying to prove to someone, anyone, that they are as good as everybody else or at least as good as the one to whom they were constantly compared. They may actually pile up impressive successes but there can never be enough, and there is no joy or satisfaction in what has been accomplished. Of course, here the emphasis is always on what they alone have done or have yet to do. An act of trusting surrender or simple acceptance of the notion that they do not have to be superhuman is out of the question. It is beyond their comprehension that it is not basically about what they do at all. It is all about what has been done for them, for us, by Christ.

To compound the problem, with the vision of "the best is yet to come" blunted or beaten out of them altogether, those wounded ones desperately seek security in arenas where it is not to be found. Frequently they tend to be obsessively negative about who they are, or who anyone else is for that matter. Success being beyond their grasp anyway, they simply drop out of the race. They never risk.

What then are they to do with this glorious invitation of Christ's to "lift up your hearts!" How in the world could they tap into the power of the meaning of Christ as the way to move from death to life? Locked within their codependency, they can hardly experience resurrection or transformation.

They may be faithfully in their place on Easter Sunday singing about the empty tomb, they may even be arrayed in new clothes for the occasion and go home to a fine Easter dinner—but they will know nothing of the true meaning of the event.

They have never experienced the call of election to come out of their own tombs; *they* have never been able to discard the funeral wrappings of their own fears and doubts; *they* have never stood beside the tomb of Lazarus and seen "Him who was dead for four days" come walking out of the gloom. And even if they had *they* would have called it a trick or found some way to discredit the marvelous event.

These recovering Catholics may or may not frequent the sacrament of the Eucharist. Whatever they do, if their codependency has taken the form of eliminating anything that is larger than life, anything like miracles popping up like popcorn, or exuberant and explosive power that hand-in-hand with the Savior allows the communicant to soar over problems and difficulties that would be unsolvable by any power on earth—then nothing is left but to munch on tiny scraps of bread and quarrel over whether that bread should be leavened or unleavened, or whether women should be allowed to touch the sacred host, or some other such nonsense.

When the meaning is lost, the only thing left to do is to founder and grope inside a bubble of worn-out ritual and symbol—or just to walk away.

INDEPENDENCE

Contrary to what many suspect, Christ did not call the children of election to mindless, childish obedience. The call constantly was to grow up, to take responsibility for our own lives. The followers were called, but it was entirely up to each individual whether or not to respond. No one is or can be forced to discipleship. Either the response to the call comes from an inner conviction or it is a cold, dead compliance.

The delicious promise of Jesus was that once the disciples took a firm hold on the Way he taught, thereby finding true security, never again would they have to give away their power to anyone or anything. These happy people are freed from the compulsion to *have* to gain the acceptance of others; they no longer had to try to fill that desperate hollow hole while sacrificing integrity for the sake of fitting in. Fitting in to what? With whom? At what price?

Knowing who they are and the source of their strength and identity, there is no need to become trapped by fad. Fads come and go. Others may endlessly chase the elusive shadow of "what's in — what's hot now," but those who know their shepherd suffer no such panic. They know. There is little else that need be said. It is the independence grounded in the content of character that Christ fostered, independence that is not afraid to consider, change, or grow. Independence that flows from a solid core need not get hung up on some basically unimportant element and then fight to the death to preserve it. There is great wisdom in being able to distinguish majors from minors. Jesus never lost sight of what really counted.

Recovering Catholics are, of course, full of stories about dropping out (not only from religion but from God) because someone who in their mind stood for God, who actually spoke for God, abused or embarrassed them over some silly or absurd issue. I am reminded of a priest who stood in the door of the church refusing entry to a Mexican migrant woman who had walked for miles to come and worship, just because she did not have a proper cloth covering her head. The man's priorities were obviously in a frightful state!

The independence that Jesus fostered, however, proven over and over in his actions and teachings, would have counseled the woman to claim what she knew, hold it fast, respond in some manner appropriate to her personality and situation, and keep right on walking with her God. Why should we let someone else, professional religious or not, and obviously in a sad state himself, dictate the conditions of our walk?

Jesus constantly invited his followers to question, examine, think, doubt. He was murdered for leading a revolt that would have stolen the power from those who made of religion a business or a front for a power base. Christ's constant questions were "Who do you say that I am? Who is the Father to you? What do you think? What makes sense to you?" His was the constant admonition to seek the God beyond—a perception of God that would reveal his very being in the whisper of the wind or the howl of the storm—if only we would listen. But that whisper or howl is meant for us. It is God speaking into our souls, not to anyone else. Not through anyone else. Not justified or validated by someone with a hierarchical title. It is ours. Within the context of a faith community, yes. Within the safety and assurance of feedback from trusted others on the journey, of course. But the message is ours. Therefore we need no other permission than our own to sojourn with our God.

CODEPENDENCY REPLIES

Once again, the fox enters the hen house! Locked into some point of negative learning, entrenched codependents find such a call to independence intolerable. Their entire life revolves around power—someone else's power. Having internalized the basic belief that they have no right to think for themselves (or the exact opposite, that *no one else* has the right to tell them anything), they are absolutely incapable of achieving the sort of peaceful independence encouraged by Christ. The only way they can put their internal machine into gear (ignoring their innate sense of how God communicates with them) is either by totally submerging their intelli-

gence and accepting the authority and opinion of someone else, or
by complete rejection of counsel from anyone.

Codependents, trapped in the conviction that their thoughts,
feelings, desires, and opinions are definitely second-rate, deserving
little or no attention, tend to store up anger like water behind a dam.
Unable to vent their rageful hurt over such treatment (at first done
to them, then the sure repetition of behaviors leading them to do it
to themselves), they simply take it, suffering the inner damage such
psychological stuffing always causes. Perpetually angry, they have
forgotten all the reasons why they are angry, yet they simply *are*
always angry. Living with this subtle yet terrible fear of "being hurt
again," they squelch and stuff and repress, turning all that energy
into inflexible attitudes, blaming others and sinking into a kind of
soul-killing negativity.

Now comes Christ saying, *Think, open up, dare to hear the
voice of God spoken just for you, just to you . . . follow that music. . .!* But those whose codependence has been like the wolf tearing
at the throat of the lamb find that unbearable. They either discount
the message, drop out entirely, or sink into the sad position of lifeless
obedience to a vacant ritual that energizes nothing. To the extent
that these recovering Catholics sit on the governing boards, make the
decisions about community policy, and direct the life of the "body
of believers," that life is in real trouble. There simply is no joy in this
kind of spirit-crushed person. Even if a minister of one kind or
another comes into their world preaching openness and attention to
an inner dialogue with God, they are incapable of hearing. Unable
to hear, of course, they can give no authentic response. Life boils
down to who is right or wrong, who does or doesn't have the clout,
who will or won't get elected, or just forget the whole business.
These are the only responses that can come from behind the barrier
of rigid, deaf, doleful codependency.

BEING VS. DOING

These conditions could well be summarized as a call to being
rather than merely doing. This has been said many times, but fo-

cusing on the reality of being is far different than simply directing our attention to what might be the proper thing to do. Doing obviously is a natural consequence of being—an honest person does not steal or lie—but a vast amount of energy and effort can be spent on observance of a law or ritual that never seems to tap into the life core of being. To say it another way: Any doing that does not reflect the state of being can be no more than a lifeless, purposeless charade.

Jesus' directions constantly urged going beyond form to substance. Sacrificing doves in the temple may have been correct procedure according to the law, but the smell of burnt sacrifice was a foul odor in his nostrils because the meaning was missing. It was a body without a heart. Stoning the woman taken in adultery may have been legal according to custom, but Jesus found it offensive. An issue far deeper than punishing the one who got caught was at stake. Jesus also seemed to take special pains to heal or eat or travel on the Sabbath, thus infuriating the powers that were. Not that there was anything wrong with the concept of the Sabbath, a day of worship, rest, prayer, and contemplation, or with the need for structure. But when it had degenerated into mere observance, it lost the anchor of meaning. Character is a function of being. Doing for the sake of doing without a pulsating, living, passionate attachment to the character that has been forged in the experiencing of God and that produces a foundation of being is hollow at best and murderous at worst.

Being provides depth. By itself, doing produces pointless activity. Being enables an open, flexible, stable security. Doing without being creates an endless flailing around for security. Being is substance. Doing without being is an amputated symbol. Being is serenity and security. Doing without being is the forlorn hope that someone "out there" will be able to locate the missing piece that has somehow managed to turn itself into a major rock in one's spiritual shoe on the trek home.

The purpose of these pages is not to protect or justify religion. The real intention here is to point out that many of the recovering Catholics, whether or not they have remained within the institution, have found immense, tragic obstacles in their pursuit of God not only because of religion, but perhaps more profoundly, because of an underlying issue of codependency that has prevented them from operating on a solid base of being. If such obstacles do indeed exist, then the occasions to flee from the garden are unlimited. Whether one opts to stay within the system or to leave it, a sweetness will always be missing, a strength will never materialize, and the call of a loving God to come walk in the cool of the evening will sound strangely off-key.

CODEPENDENCY REPLIES

Anyone who has followed the reasoning thus far will plainly see that all negative codependent imprinting is an assault upon the formation of a healthy being. All codependency is about the loss of identity and independence. It is also about the giving up of our power to decide appropriately, thus giving others the right to decide whether we are good enough or not, right or not, acceptable or not. Codependency is infallibly about boundaries. The deeper the codependency the less the individual is able to establish healthy boundaries around a host of issues: How much is enough? What are my rights? When is guilt appropriate? Who do I have to be to be good enough? Who is the judge of that? When is it time to move on, to stop straddling the fence? Such codependency in all its forms stands directly in the way of one seeking the path of Christ and muffles the constant call to being, to "hold your head up and remember who you are."

To Walk More Fully in the Light

Many and understandable are the reasons to discard religion as a somewhat quaint relic of the past, when the generalized term *religion* becomes reduced to a specific religious community or parish that seems to manifest precious few of those desirable traits we have already discussed, or worse, a particular religious community that has caused harm in some direct, personal way.

To emphasize as strongly as possible, no matter what our problems with religion, they need not destroy our relationship with God. Religion, spirituality, and God are not all the same reality! While we may have been told, or indeed have felt that a specific problem was of religious or faith origin, it may have roots in a codependency problem. This may cause gross and unfixable spiritual problems if not recognized and healed.

Codependency breeds hypersensitivity and the tendency to overreact. As with all overreaction, what we are responding to is not the present issue, the one in the here and now, but some hidden issue buried within, back in the there and then. It is the old wound reaching out from the past infecting each new day. Codependency, which is centered around the abuse of power, will project and act out that hurt in monstrous proportions in the politics of a parish community. Anyone whose codependency has turned trust into a furtive dash down a thug-infested street will rebel at any invitation to vulnerability or community. Such people will fight to the death, solidly convinced of the justification of their cause, to keep things "proper," which may really mean sanitized of any interpersonal exchange in the community.

Another who has been damaged around the right to make mistakes and has stored up megatons of anger over all those painful lessons may violently overreact so that a benign and innocent suggestion of some well-intentioned effort is immediately perceived as hostile criticism. Perhaps it was more a poor choice of words from the one making the remark, but in the exaggerated economy of codependency it was "another" intolerable slap in the face. Coattails flap in the breeze as such people flee from any further contact with "them."

Religion is and always will be flawed, but if we are ever to emerge into the light more fully, we must identify the problem correctly. And that problem may well not be weak faith but strong codependency. As we will discuss later, though these are related, they are very different realities that yield to different technologies. Codependency will not vanish simply through prayer or fasting, and certainly not through simply trying harder! How many perfectionists, workaholics, and martyrs have ground themselves to powder attempting this method of healing!

Healing

Healing is made up of many elements,
it is mysterious, unclocked,
following its own course and rules.
Yet when it has happened it is known.
We do not depart from a healing
the same as when we came. We have been changed.
Whenever existence has truly been shared,
there is a measure of healing—or conversion.
Anger melts to peace,
hostility to compassion,
resentment to forgiveness.
That which was lost, the lost child in all of us,
at least in part is found.
There can be no healing without finding,
and no real finding without love,
for it is love, surrounding the finding,
that makes it safe to see what we have seen.
To ask the question is already to know the answer.
It just might not be safe to admit it, own it.
Love makes it safe—perhaps not easy but safe.

• 4 •

Community: The Breaking of the Bread

Of all the major religions in the world, none places more emphasis on community than Christianity. The followers of Christ are bound together both in spirit and doctrine to function within the bounds of community. Every miracle Christ performed was for the sake of the community, not just for individual healing or edification. After the transfiguration, the apostles were forbidden to remain hiding on the mountain, marveling over their wondrous experience. Their commission was to return to the world of humankind and build the Kingdom, always expressed in the form of community. Each of the sacraments so central to the functioning of Christianity is structured as a communal event.

This brings to mind that well-known Shakespearian gem, "Ah, there is the rub." The goal may be community yet the disappointment of so many Christians today is precisely that lack of genuine community. All too often what is acted out in the name of religion feels like a charade. Buildings called churches, filled with people going through the motions of worship but having no real knowledge of any fellow worshipers, no sharing, no opportunity or even desire to get involved with each other, is scarcely a valid concept of community.

The primitive word for "church" itself, *ecclesia*, does not mean a building on a street at which more or less mandatory, often boring rites are performed. The word means "a community of believers." It has nothing to do with brick and mortar. The church is wherever and whenever true believers gather to celebrate a central event in their lives, an event teeming with meaning and power.

In the history of the contemporary church, the hunt for what-ever constitutes true community has generated enormous efforts. Most recently, following the Second Vatican Council, which em-phasized ministry as community building and faith as a personal relationship with Christ rather than intellectual assent to a mountain of dogma, the search was on again.

Since then, with much good will and great sincerity, many attempts have been made to found community on guitar music, coffee klatches, encounter groups, sensationalism, or reverting to tradition, such as saying the Mass in Latin again—in general a bend-ing over backward to fit religion into the life-style and convenience of possible attendees. Noble efforts all, yet ultimately doomed to failure. Christian community simply cannot be founded on anything else but the radical, soul-burning experience of an encounter with the living presence of Jesus Christ.

I shudder even as I write these words to recovering Catholics. For many in the Roman Church, phraseology such as "a personal experience of Christ" smacks of dangerous or even cultish theology. Or if not that, so much emphasis on personal experience is just not the "way we do it." Yet think about it. Any true community, vibrant with enthusiasm, not bogged down in minutia, is built around some central, life-changing experience. From that experience, genuine commitment flows. And from that commitment grows structure that promotes life rather than strangling it. That experience and the sub-sequent commitment generate symbols and rituals bursting with meaning, not a moribund compliance. Those who have shared in that experience have a true fellowship that goes beyond words—understood without endless explanation. Cost or personal inconven-ience is not an issue when tasks or opportunities present themselves to further the cause of the movement built around that central event.

A recent illustration, whatever one's political persuasion, was Operation Desert Storm. Simply to be able to say, "I was there," places one in a special arena of shared experience, commitment, and status. Anyone who participated in that event enters the rank of a special community.

Community, of course, comes in many depths and descriptions. The thousands of people at a rock concert could be called a community—or consider a stadium full of excited fans at a big homecoming game. They are certainly bound by a common experience. Often neighborhoods or certain geographic areas are called communities simply because they all live in close proximity even though the vast majority of people in that space may go out of their way *not* to know each other.

Christian community, however, is a different and very specific kind of thing. The sort of community to which Christ called his followers has at its very core a prerequisite if membership is to have any substantial meaning or power. That prerequisite is a personal encounter with Christ. In some real way Christ must have made a difference in the content and direction of the life of each member if there is to be any sense in coming together to celebrate the existence of that experience.

People who hate music in general and rock music in particular can still go to a rock concert. What's to stop them? But for such persons the experience would be boring at best and torture at worst. They are not believers.

Those who think "football is just a gang of brutish boys running around jumping on a defenseless ball," as a British friend of mine once remarked, may certainly get involved in the enthusiasm of a homecoming game. They may enjoy all the energy, but there is something seriously missing in their involvement. It just isn't the same as it might be for the people sitting next to them who have actually played the game or in some way had their core touched by what is going on in front of them. There is something about having played the game that makes all the difference. Even forty years later, the memory of having been in a fourth-and-one situation, knowing that the man across the line, at that very moment, is willing to commit murder to move you that one yard off the line, tends to leave its mark. And you, being equally willing to do whatever it takes not to be moved, make of this homecoming game, so many years later, an instant replay.

The old scars start to throb, the blood boils. Memory, always slanting things in your direction, becomes not a static picture of the past, but a living, breathing, in-your-face event, taking place right before your very eyes. The memory of someone sticking their fingers through your face mask trying to slow you down, or taking a bite out of your leg (or other body parts in some big pile up), gives you an insider's sense of the game that mere spectators can never know. The one can only be a spectator, the other a true fan. One must either have been there as a participant or been able to transfer a similar experience to gain entrance to the inner meaning of the game. And so it is with one's walk with Christ.

What else could possibly be at the core of a community built around the name Christian if not an experience of Christ? That encounter, of course, is as varied, as different in nuance and expression as there are different shades of green in Ireland. God speaks to us in a manner unique to each of us, but speak he does, and the quality of our openness to that call, the manner of our response, will dictate the depth of the encounter. That encounter then will dictate the quality of the community that comes together to celebrate exactly that exchange between God and his people.

Entrance into the early Christian communities required a long, intensive catechumenate, often consisting of a year of education and nurture before these adults were admitted to the full community through the sacrament of baptism. Today, the mere ritual of baptism hardly ensures that there has been any such experience of Christ, especially since most baptisms are infant intensive! Just because people have been baptized does not mean that they have stood shoulder to shoulder with Christ in some dark hour, it does not mean that they have felt the saving grace of having been lifted up when they reached out; it doesn't mean at all that they ever have or do now walk in the cool of the evening with their friend and Savior.

Over the years different sacraments may mark our lives—baptism, confirmation, learning how to go to confession, being married "in the church" replete with lovely pomp and ceremony. But none of that necessarily provides or indicates any experience of a living, powerful, loving God. Even if the memories down that religious road are mostly positive, even if our hearts warm at the thought of the cloud of incense filling a quiet church during benediction or if getting gold stars for memorizing catechism questions was a real highlight of our youth, all well and good, but those fond memories in and of themselves say nothing at all of knowing Christ. Knowing about perhaps yes, but actually knowing Christ, no. Spectators are a very different breed from fans.

A sense of what this encounter is like is found throughout Scripture, but it is especially clear in the last pages of the Gospel of Luke. Christ is dead and the disciples are in a terrible stew about what to do next. Their souls are flat, their energy drained. As of yet they have had no set-you-on-fire experience of the risen Christ. Then—he stands in their midst.

He asks them why they are so downhearted, why so confused. Their fear and apathy are so unattractive even a man dying of thirst would hardly think to ask a drink of water from them! Patiently, Christ explains to them the meaning of the Scriptures—that he had to die in order to rise from the dead and live again. "Why are you so agitated, why these doubts rising in your minds?" he asks. "Look at my hands and feet—yes, it is I indeed. Touch me and see for yourselves" (Luke 24:38–39). And they did touch him. That is the heart of it. They touched. That touch was apparently like fire. Then Christ promised them the Spirit and sent them on their way, filled with joy! They certainly were not the same persons as before they were confronted with the living Christ. They were changed— forever. Their fears, doubts, and anxieties were lifted from them. As a powerful minister recently told me, "They became miracle-minded!"

To know Christ is to know that life is stronger than death. The business of Christ is always about conquering death. A community that forms around such an experience is always about the business of transformation. Not just information. Transformation. Information can only become transformation through the process of internalization. Internalization requires processing. It is in this processing—the praying for openness, the sharing, the being in the fellowship of others who have been touched by the fire—that those codependent callouses are slowly rubbed off; the doors fling open, and the mud is washed from the windows.

Whatever in religion and religious community is of God is simply God's business. But that part of it that is human requires constant attention and the tools that humans need for healing and improvement. Internalizing facts about God until they become a life lived with God requires a community involvement. The human story, our story, is the "stuff" of what all this effort and energy is about. Our lives are the clay on the potter's wheel of the Spirit. The molding hands of others have a lot to do with what that precious lump of clay turns out to be. After all, it is those "others" who have largely influenced recovering Catholics either to shut down in their pews or just drop out altogether. The question is, of course—what is the quality of those hands that shape the clay of our lives? Is the touch gentle? Wise? Loving? Is there a life that flows through those hands that is connected to a higher, brighter life beyond and within? Pity fresh clay at the mercy of stone hands!

It is well said that "holy" means any place where it is safe to tell one's story. This is a thought well worth considering. Our stories are our lives. Life as it is played out in each of our special, unique scenarios is what Christ came to make better. Our life stories are the focal points of redemption as it applies to us. They are where all the action is. The knowing and telling of our stories, how touching the face of God has impacted those stories of ours is what all the fuss is about. The whole point of community is to protect, enhance, and celebrate the treasure that each of our stories is. To be out of touch with our stories or never to have a chance to share them and learn from others is equivalent to the ancient Israelites being told they must make bricks without straw. Take away the main ingredient and what is left? Christian communities must be places where it is safe to tell our stories.

Many have fled our communities because they were not safe places to be. They have found acceptance and welcome in places one would never think of. An older gentleman I know never fails to spend his afternoons at a local mall where he sits with his cronies drinking coffee and "telling lies about the past" as he calls it. Certainly it is a community of sorts. Another powerful community based on the need for a common, central life-changing experience if ever there is to be genuine community is found in the fellowship of recovery of Alcoholics Anonymous and other Twelve-Step organizations. There is much in the recovering communities that parallels and models all that is or could be so immensely powerful in church communities. Not that everyone in A.A. is a saint or even on the road to recovery. Far from it. But radiating from the core of the true believers is a sense that their lives have been saved from ruin. They were dead and came back to life through a spiritual conversion and the fellowship of other A.A. members. All of them know what it means to teeter on the brink of disaster, to be utterly without hope or even any right to hope—yet now they live.

At its best, in A.A., as in all true communities, there is never a question of "why am I here?" There is never a complaint of "ah, gee, do I have to go to another meeting?" At its best, there is a burning desire to "carry the message" to other suffering alcoholics. That burning desire is kindled white hot from the personal experience of having been dead and yet finding there is indeed a way to return to the living.

A Dream Team

Consider a present-day church community, a dream team, made up of these characters:

Lazarus: the brother of Martha and Mary who was dead for four days before Christ called him back from the grave (John 11:17–44 NEB).

Jairus: the father of the girl at death's door, whom Christ told to return home because his daughter had been healed (Luke 8:40–56 NEB).

The Leper: one of the ten whom Christ healed, but the only one who returned to thank him for what he had done (Luke 17:11–19 NEB).

The Adulterous Woman: the one Jesus saved from stoning by standing up for her in the face of the power brokers of the day (John 8:2–11 JB).

Zacchaeus: the hated tax collector whom Jesus called down from a tree where he was watching, telling him he would be staying with him that day, causing a major conversion in the man (Luke 19:1–10 JB).

The Blind Man healed on the Sabbath: having been healed by Jesus on the forbidden day, he was hauled in to appear before the Pharisees. They badgered the poor man, demanding to know who this man was, and what right he had to do this "work" on the Sabbath. The healed man simply replied, "I only know that I was blind and now I can see" (John 9:24–26 JB).

Somehow I just can't imagine this group complaining about a bunch of Al-Anon folks using their coffee pot!

Think of the power of these people! Consider their single-minded focus when they gathered to celebrate the meal of the Lord. Imagine sitting next to them when it came time to sing or to share a sign of peace or, would that it could ever happen, to share an experience of the power of God in their lives. What community they would have—without guitars or coffee or even bingo! A community begun on the inside, expressing itself magnetically on the outside. First a matter of being, then and only then, a matter of doing.

The late contemporary Jewish leader, Rabbi Heschel, constantly urged the Jewish community to be aware of "Kavanah"—a return to the inner meaning, the inside of our being, focusing on the intent of what we are saying or praying, not just mumbling words by rote. Ritual and symbol devoid of an inside meaning are simply dead ritual and symbol.

How can we discover this inner meaning? What is its core? What is its power?

For the Christian community, nothing will suffice but that each of us, in our own way and with our own needs, discovers the power of death to life in union with Jesus Christ. Once this experience has been identified and celebrated not only through intellectual teachings but truly shared verbally with others in faith, genuine community begins to form. This kind of community is not built on popular fad or what fits at the moment. Much of the radical call of Jesus to discipleship does not fit. That which is new, hot, or convenient may well be nothing more than shifting sand, which makes a pretty lousy foundation to build upon. But a community founded on nothing less than an encounter of the third kind with Christ—as with our dream team—oozes with power.

In his instructions to Peter, Jesus promised that the gates of hell would not prevail against the community of his church. The tense of the verb in this passage denotes the active voice, not the passive. Christ was saying that when the community is solidly based in the power of God, the commission then is to take that community and actively crash it into the gates of hell, and those gates will fold every time. Hardly a passive suggestion that no matter how badly hell pounds on the doors of the community, it will not be knocked out. Quite the opposite. The commission, as it was to Abraham and Moses to pick up their staffs and get moving, is still the same. The reason for the church to exist is hardly to fight over coffee pots. The reason is to confront the darkness and show that light really wins.

Rhetoric? Sermonizing? Nice words in a cruel world?

Precisely the point. Only those who have been rescued from the shadow of death, and only those who have recognized that union with Christ truly does take a person to a new level, truly does make a difference, ever get down to the real meaning and business of Christian community. Only they do not fall victim to siphoning off their energy, quibbling about matters that do not amount to a hill of beans. Within the communities we call churches, if lives are not being saved, physically as well as emotionally and spiritually, then what of any consequence is going on?

The sequence is conversion, commitment, community. Then, look out! The power of God will turn up the most unexpected miracles. This kind of community will never be short of throngs of people seeking to join. A true faith community is a veritable miracle factory. Anyone familiar with this kind of living, breathing extension of the Body of Christ, knows that the faces are different. The faces of those touched by this fire glow. Truly, the faces shine.

One Was a Plumber, One Was a Lawyer, and Another a Nurse

Is this experience of Christ so difficult? Is it reserved only for an elite few? Only for saints or addicts or others who have "hit bottom"? If this is the case, have we not just limited the membership in our communities to a point where they will cease to exist?

The fact is that nearly all of us have had many and wondrous experiences of God in our lives that could serve as a foundation for vibrant faith and community living, but we have failed to recognize them. Once identified, we can nurture these God touches, coax them into revealing their secrets, celebrate them as the "real stuff," and use them in turn to liberate other stories of the splendor of "God-with-us."

For most, it is exactly at this juncture that the road becomes the most slippery. I am suggesting that our lives have been and continue to be full of marvelous burning-bush experiences if only we would stop to notice and identify them as such.

Working with various church renewal groups, many times I have addressed these words to what seemed like an endless sea of faces, only to be met with polite, skeptical expressions. The following simple technique often made a great deal of difference:

First, I broke them into small groups and asked them to introduce themselves by telling their fellow group members how they happened to be part of this particular church community and what they would most like to see happen in their own particular church.

Almost visibly, walls transformed into bridges. Perhaps these people had been acquainted, had even served on the same committees or had just "seen each other around" for the past ten years or so. Often, so often they were never in a situation that allowed them to meet one another on any human or personal level.

Next I would explain the difference between a discussion and a faith sharing. Discussions, more often than not, are about right and wrong, or at least "righter," and frequently degenerate into a contest of who is the smartest, the swiftest, or the biggest bully—a veritable breeding ground for codependency.

Faith sharing, on the other hand, has no right or wrong, it is simply what has been our experience—our stories. No one knows more about a person's story than that person does, so all the fear of appearing stupid, not getting it right, being in competition, or being laughed at are swept away. The potter's wheel is being prepared to shape life's most beautiful art.

I would then present this question: Recall an experience when you felt the closest to God, when you most clearly heard God whisper in your ear, when you felt that gentle embrace. When was the last time you met the burning bush?

Shock, or at the very least, doubt often registered. Obviously, this question would be more appropriate for saints. God talking to us? The following answer came from quite a memorable group, half in play perhaps, but tinged with seriousness, "Gee, one of us is a lawyer, one a plumber, and one a nurse—we're just ordinary people." What could they possibly have to do with burning bushes or even all that stuff about walking in the cool of the evening for that matter?

But they, like all the others, were encouraged to settle down, release their fear because this was not a competition, no grades would be given, no golden stars plastered on foreheads. They were just asked to reflect quietly, with pencil and paper at hand, and write down a time, any time, when they felt they were on holy ground. If feasible, the lights would be lowered a bit, some soothing music played. Soon miracles started popping. Sooner or later, in this setting, pencils would fairly race across the pages, faces would begin to shine. I have never seen it fail.

After an appropriate amount of time, I would gather them back into their groups and ask them to share (faith-share) with each other what they had discovered about that Hidden Presence in their lives. "Tell your story," they were encouraged.

The stories of how God speaks to each of us in a special way began to unfold. There were heart-tugging accounts of the moment of the birth of a child—or a child's death. Some told of being in the pit of a personal tragedy when a tiny ray of sunshine pierced the darkest cloud, and for no reason they could perceive, in one blessed moment came a thought or an idea or perhaps just an abiding sense that eventually something good would come of it. For others it was simply the experience of being with friends or family when they most felt the presence of God. There were tales of quiet, personal times alone in the mountains or walking by the sea when the Divine was most powerfully felt. One man spoke simply of walking among his flowers and sensing God smiling at him.

The stories were always endlessly varied and uniformly beautiful. When the renewal schedule covered several days, much of the remaining time was spent in other such faith-sharing events. A powerful variation is to ask each participant to pick a favorite passage of Scripture and then translate it into their own lives. They are asked to elaborate on how and why that particular passage means what it does to them, what experience it ties into that gives it such deep personal meaning. The Scriptures leap to life! All, as was meant to be, become experts in their own right, experts as to how and why this event or truth from Scripture has touched their lives. No one can be more expert on their lives than they themselves.

Again, if the event lasted several days, the members were encouraged to carry small notebooks in order to jot down events during the day when they heard the "bush crackle." Inevitably, once awareness sets in, the face of God appears everywhere. The question never is, is God there? The question is, do we have the eyes to see? Spurred on by the faith sharing of the group—never a competition— the participants become more "sighted." Faith sighted.

The next step is to initiate dialogue, based on the experiences that they have shared, about the purpose and direction their community should pursue—how all the pieces that make up a parish fit. Then comes some introspection about what their particular piece contributes to the whole and what and how other "pieces" contribute to the picture. Exactly as solid as this experience of Christ is in their lives, and the extent to which it remains uppermost in their spirits, to that extent the entire community will be solidly Christ-centered. Such Christ awareness is the single element that can save a community from shipwrecking on the boulders of petty politics and drowning in minutia.

Elements Necessary for a Dynamite Community

1. An experience of Christ must be identified and celebrated.

2. A concept of community will then emerge, a coming together that will include a vision of the whole. The reason for church will become clear—to create an environment most inviting to others to experience and then share in this same fundamental experience. It is this vision that eliminates "kingdom mentality," the scourge of so many Christian communities. Kingdom mentality is the belief that "my part of this pie is all that counts, whether finances, liturgy, kids, education, or mission, and I will fight to the death to defend my little kingdom no matter what it does to the whole."

3. Community will form based on the understanding that there is no such thing as "big" community. There are only small communities that come together. Those small communities are based on the sharing, helping, and bonding together of weaknesses to form strengths on which all real community is founded. A stadium of ten thousand people can be a community if they have shared a common, important experience and then come together to celebrate and share again in its meaning. Two people in a cathedral, present out of fear or routine, surrounded by centuries of pomp and pageantry but with no shared experience or involvement with each other, are just two strangers who happen to be in the same place at the same time. The mere fact of being in a church at a particular service does not necessarily make a community celebration any more than just being in a garage makes you a car.

Amazing Grace at Emmaus

A most touching story from the primitive church is recounted at the tail end of the Gospel of Luke. Two disciples, Cleopas and a friend, are heading out of Jerusalem two days after Christ's death. We are not told why they are hurrying to the village of Emmaus some seven miles from Jerusalem, but the sense of the story is that they were not dawdling.

As they hustle along, they are talking about what is uppermost on their minds, what happened to Jesus. As of yet they have not encountered the power of the risen Christ. True, they heard his promises, they learned a great deal of dogma from the Scriptures, they witnessed the tragedy of the crucifixion, and they no doubt have been going to church all their lives. But they have not met the risen Christ.

They continue to stride along, heads down, lost before the Light, when a stranger approaches. Innocently, he asks what they are talking about. Astonished and apparently a bit irritated, they respond that he must be the only person in Jerusalem who doesn't know what has been going on. What planet does he live on? Only a clod wouldn't know that Christ the prophet has been murdered. And to make matters even worse, some of the women went to the tomb and claimed they found it empty! What could have happened to his body? Had the Romans played some dirty trick or was it a gross and dastardly act of vandalism? We can just hear the wheels whirring!

The stranger made a rather pointed remark about how dull they were and then, starting from Moses, he explained the Scriptures to them even up to this present time, pointing out that the Christ had to die in order that life might be set free. When they reached the village, he made as if to go on, but the two men were so impressed that they begged him to stay with them and share their evening meal. Still, they did not recognize Christ nor taste of his Life. Only in the blessing and breaking of the bread did their eyes open. Only then did they not only understand but also were touched by what they understood. They not only saw the Light, they became the light. Only after they tasted of the Bread and that Bread became flesh of their flesh and bone of their bone did they pack up and head straight back to Jerusalem to gather in community with the other disciples and share their experience.

How like old Cleopas and his partner are so many of us who call ourselves Christians. Informed. Schooled. Erudite. Knowing all about the promise, walking as far as the hill of the crucifixion but somehow never taking the next step—experiencing the resurrection. Christ's story does not end with death. That is the whole point. That is what makes all the effort and struggle worth it. Life conquers death. Until, however, we experience the kind of amazing grace that happened on the road to Emmaus, there is nothing left for any Christian or Christian community but to wander around learned and empty. Or unlearned and empty. But empty all the same. Empty does not change the world. Empty does not crash into the gates of hell and come out victorious. Empty desperately tries to find something—anything—around which to build community. And that something or anything ultimately and invariably fails.

The fact remains that the condition and direction of the community will inevitably reflect its experience of Christ. If that experience is superficial then all that flows from it will be clearly expressed in the communal setting. Parish meetings will degenerate into politics; ritual, no matter how fancy or with how much fanfare, will resemble putting a brand new suit on a corpse; outreach, undertaken with enormous good will and energy, will be unable to go the distance. After all sorts of work, its legs will simply give out.

If the encounter with Christ has been twisted into a sort of horror movie, perhaps a version of the little kid meeting the monster, then that too will be reflected in the community life. Certainly there will be much activity. But activity based on fear is not what the disciples felt when they rushed back from Emmaus. There is not even a hint that they returned to their fellow disciples with a warning to shape up and perform or all they knew of hell would resemble a marshmallow roast. Faces simply do not glow when fear lurks at the heart of the matter. Christians dance with joy—fear produces a terrified shivering in the dark. No one who operates out of the fear that

God might kill their children or visit them with cancer or just turn them into frogs because of their misdeeds, has ever met the risen Christ.

Throughout the centuries, people have tried bartering—going to church or "being good" because of a perception that religion is some kind of business deal where God can be persuaded to look the other way. This turns out to be more of an insurance policy than anything else. The idea here is that if we do all these "good" things, then when we die (if there is a God), we won't go to hell (if there is a hell), but instead we will go to heaven (if there is a heaven) even though sitting around on clouds playing a harp throughout eternity doesn't sound like all that much fun.

Belief with a "Kavanah" kind of commitment has nothing whatsoever to do with religion as business. Commitment isn't about insurance or playing it safe. As freely as a waterfall, commitment flows from an encounter with the living Christ, being moved from the inside out by a need that will not be denied. It is a song from the depth of one's being that can no more be stilled or suppressed than the look of absolute wondrous love on a mother's face as she gazes at her newborn baby.

Anything real is born from a personal encounter with meaning—something that shakes the soul and leaves the individual forever changed, forever different. Anyone else who has shared a like experience becomes a brother or sister in a fashion that makes even blood relationships pale by comparison.

An example of this process, although tragic, jumped at me when I recently attended a gathering of MADD (Mothers Against Drunk Driving). No questions here, no doubts, no ambiguities, no forced attendance. Everybody there knew exactly why they were there. They knew the very insides of each other. From their sharing came enormous strength, healing, and wisdom. They were truly there for each other. The breaking of the bread within, by which they recognized one another, was the sorrow and grief of their senseless loss and the desperate desire to do whatever they could to prevent other such tragedies. No question at all about their mission.

"Real" swirls like a mist around The Wall in Washington, D.C. You can cut it with a knife. The letters, flowers, and symbols left there are enough to shred the soul. Many times the collective heart and mind of an entire nation have been stirred by watching a buddy or a loved one tenderly touching a cold carved name, and through that touch, empowered by the experience behind it, somehow passing beyond granite to warm, living flesh and blood. It would be an unthinkable national sacrilege to hold a boisterous drunken picnic beside The Wall. Can we imagine being there in the presence of such profound meaning, perhaps someone searching out the name of a son or spouse, and impatiently glancing at our watch, wondering just how long this will take? Or can we contemplate refusing to allow people to approach The Wall, people who want to touch a loved one, because their heads were not correctly covered?

Ridiculous concepts. Made more so because of the depth and profundity of the meaning that lies behind and within that cold, black granite. The Wall is a symbol, and the job of a symbol is to convey meaning. The symbol can be no more powerful in energizing or bonding a community than the meaning that the participants bring to it.

In the case of the Eucharist—that fundamental experience of touching the risen Christ nestled in the very heart of the Mass, that binding ritual of thanksgiving for the disciples, the early community of believers—much of the early meaning and substance remains present today whether or not anyone recognizes it. But let that amazing grace be touched again in the present day, and that particular community will proclaim a common and Kavanah purpose—to glorify Christ by creating an environment where the miracle of death turning into life is a daily occurrence for any who would accept it. There will be a common and Kavanah language—liturgies will be from the heart and no one will exhort the priest to "make it short, the game starts in half an hour." There will be a common and Kavanah mission—to seek each and every opportunity to light the fire wherever two pieces of wood are to be found. They will know what they are doing and why—because they were there!

It may well be true that many recovering Catholics have fled because this kind of a community, or even a faint shadow of it, was nowhere to be found. Of course, it may be equally true that they themselves did little or nothing to establish a more loving community. Perhaps they came only to take, never to give. Perhaps at that time in their lives, when they came seeking community, they *had* nothing to give. Or it may well be that they gave it all they had, but either owing to the amount of codependency strangling their freedom or the massive inertia of dried-out tradition or the dispirited state of the leadership in their community—or for a host of other reasons, they left. Exhausted, disappointed, enraged, crushed, hopeless, whatever—they left. And many felt that when they walked away, they had to leave God behind as well.

While God is not religion, nor religious community, nor dogma about God, all of these realities can and should augment and amplify the music coming from the garden, the music inviting us to walk in the cool of the evening with that fellow traveler made known to us in the breaking of the bread.

Obstacles

Let us examine four obstacles that prevent the formation of this kind of community.

CODEPENDENCY

If codependency is a major obstacle to experiencing the call of Christ and making an appropriate response, by that very fact it is an obstacle to the building of a Christ-centered community. Whatever prevents the individual encounter with Christ becomes a thief at the core of community.

Trust underlies all successful relationships. It doesn't take a world-class psychologist to grasp the fact that when most or even many members of a given community lack the ability to trust, no matter how lofty the intellectual foundation or eloquent the mission statement, very little will take place that resembles the Emmaus meal. Community is a spider web of interlocking relationships. The whole can only be as strong as the combined strength of the separate relationships of which it consists.

Vulnerability will never be risked without trust. Without vulnerability, access is denied to the inner dimensions of the human heart, which is where Christ seeks to pitch his tent. Codependency guards the lock on the gate to that inner garden where life rises up out of death.

A Christian community lacking the grand vision of how life could and should unfold in a marvelous manner is a contradiction in terms. A community made up of people who are negative-minded, who get lost in trivia, whose faces don't shine, is simply not able to create life-giving structures. Every community must have structure. The question then becomes whether these structures are an end unto themselves, or whether, due to that underlying grand vision, they become connecting rods that enable the power of God to pass back and forth between Creator and creature.

Vision is light. Light is wisdom. Wisdom is life giving. If we don't dare to dream, to stretch beyond the length of our arms and the outer edges of our minds to a higher level, how shall we ever come to know or celebrate him who makes all things possible?

The skills that enable the individual to connect with Christ are also crucial to a community if it is to be truly Christ-centered. The technology of recovery that has developed over the last several decades dealing with codependency and its satellite concerns (working with the inner child, healing shame, understanding Family of Origin imprinting) offers new tools of enormous import for building Christian community. Their use can prevent the loss of many disenchanted Christians while enabling desperately needed, genuine homecomings. Communities able to provide this technology in one fashion or another have gone far toward solving their community problems. However it is approached, effective ways to deal with the deadly effect of codependency need to be found.

Loss of Focus

For many communities, mere survival has become the focus. Raising the funds just to keep the doors open absorbs all the effort and energy of leaders and followers alike. The community may direct its endeavors to keeping a school functioning or to the support of some other grand cause or project. Survival can be a mighty motivator. Specific just and important causes can be powerful rallying points. Yet if the focus of the Christian community is other than leading individuals to a knowing of Christ in their own lives and a celebration of that living presence in their midst, the path becomes treacherous indeed. First being—then doing.

Over the centuries, many major and minor crimes have been committed in the name of Christ. That is precisely why there is such a great need for honest, codependency-free communities, acting as a sounding board for all that is exchanged in the community and providing a trustworthy map to guide its future journey.

When mere observance of ritual and tradition become the focus, and "being correct" replaces "metanoia," communities become riderless horses. Christ was much more concerned with being real than being correct. Real not in the current slang sense, but real in the sense of being concerned with the quality of our lives, marching into our innermost chambers, casting out the darkness, opening the windows, sweeping away the cobwebs. Christ always sought to reach behind dull eyes, push aside the mask and delve right into the real live human heart beating away. Such a focus has little to do with being correct or cautious. When we point the arrow of our life directly at the heart of God and then loose the bowstring, we find that it will infallibly fly to the heart of humanity as well. Our focus remains true.

Misplaced Priorities

Obviously if the true focus is obscured, perhaps to the point of obliteration, there will be precious little to promote the seeking out and following of what all the excitement was about in the first place.

The basic priority of conversion, and the right of everyone, indeed the call of everyone to that experience simply will not be heard. "Heard," of course, takes on many forms. The most obvious is heard, as in the spoken word. Preaching. If meeting Christ and becoming united with God is not part and parcel of the preached word, and if that word does not radiate the power of someone who has "been there," then obviously much of what Christian community is meant to have, to be, and to offer will be missing.

There is also a much more subtle sense of "heard." By this I mean heard in the way that a group of committed people who gather together seem to radiate a central meaning, a purpose and direction, with gentle yet very real passion. To be around such a company of believers—either believers in a certain sports team or some avocation—is to be pulled in, wrapped up, surrounded by whatever shaped that belief. Their enthusiasm is infectious.

Once I accidentally spent several hours on a bus in the midst of half a dozen rock hounds returning from a mineralogical show. By the time we parted, I was ready to get a pick and shovel and head for the hills. There had been no arm twisting, no fiery sermons, certainly no threats of dire consequences if I didn't follow suit. The attraction was the excitement they exuded over what was obviously very beautiful and powerful in their lives. There is no way we can conceal what we deeply believe, for it will radiate from us. Whether the belief is negative or positive, we constantly send out ripples that set other ripples into motion.

When a community is founded on a deep experience of Christ, the countless ways in which the Lord chooses to initiate those encounters will be made known. They underlie facial expression, body language, tone of voice, and, perhaps most of all, the serenity of a peaceful life. A life truly built on the security that comes from intimate knowledge of God is a noisy life indeed, a life that is "heard."

LACK OF LEADERSHIP

The life of any community takes its cue from its leader or leaders. The pulpit is the core of every Christian community. The level of spirituality of the community will be determined by the level of spirituality coming from the spoken word emanating from that pulpit. Rarely is the spirituality of the community greater than the spirituality of the pulpit. If an encounter with Christ is the key note of authentic religion and this encounter is critical for the individual, then how much more so for the one who stands at the center of the community that exists to celebrate such an experience.

As we will discuss in greater detail in the following chapter, the key to leadership is not just gaining more professional skills or techniques. The key is that the leader of the community has been and is walking in the cool of the evening with the God whom he or she has met in the depths of the soul.

That You May Be One

A hundred or so years ago when I conducted many retreats for teenagers, I often used an exercise that never failed to raise goose bumps. It was called simply "the Emmaus meal."

Of course it took some time to get the kids quieted down, minus their perpetual tape recorders and non-stop talking, but eventually they were persuaded to turn inward a bit, and just listen. Not to me, but to themselves. The idea was to introduce them to the concept that quiet, rather than being the world's worst torture, could become one's greatest friend. They were being invited to hear in the silence that which they could never hear, and therefore never know, unless they were quiet.

That rather monumental task having been more or less accomplished, I asked them to write down on a piece of paper their deepest need. Perhaps one or two of them. They were assured that this would be kept totally anonymous, and they would not have to read aloud what they had written. Whatever they put on that paper would be the silent song from their innermost heart. (Little did they know that I knew, from having done this hundreds of times, pretty much what they would write. With mighty few exceptions, it always came out the same.)

Next, they were asked to fold their papers to ensure privacy and one by one approach a table upon which was placed a long loaf of French bread. There was a reading from Scripture explaining that to partake of the bread was to take on the responsibility of caring for one another. To eat of the bread and drink of the cup was to signify a willingness to enter into a community, founded upon the person and spirit of Jesus, who commanded that we love one another. Who prayed that we all might be one as He and the Father were one. Who told us that as He was loved by the Father so were we loved by Him and in that love we were to make sure that no one among us lived as a forgotten, abandoned child. No one living within the community of Jesus was allowed to live with the belief that they were junk.

As the young people left their folded papers containing their deepest needs, they were in turn given a piece of the bread. Eventually everyone had a small chunk of the bread. Then the papers were redistributed among the participants. They all ended up with someone else's paper. They all, rather wide-eyed when they realized what they held, stood there with that piece of bread in one hand and the deepest need of someone else in the other.

The account of the Emmaus event was then read, how in the breaking of the bread their eyes were opened and they recognized Christ with them, full of light and life. The youngsters were then told that what they held in one hand *was* what they held in the other. The bread was not just bread but the living, breathing needs and hurts and hopes and beauty of each person in that room. It is safe to say that as they then consumed their bread, they did so with a new awareness of what such a statement meant.

Throughout the remainder of the retreat, they carried those papers around with them. Supposedly they had neither looked at nor shared its contents with their special buddies. Fat chance! At the closing liturgy they were given the opportunity to decide whether or not they wanted to share what was on their paper with the group. Of course they always did. For one thing, it wasn't their paper and for another who wants to keep anything like that to themselves? Besides, everyone within a fifty-mile radius already knew what it said.

Those needs were always variations of the same thing: to be accepted, to have a really good friend, no longer to have to prove themselves, not to feel so alone. As Carl Jung observed many years ago—that which is most personal is also most common.

Although this technique is simple, its meaning is not limited to teenagers. In this increasingly complex, pressured, and frequently scary world, we all need to belong, we all need acceptance but not priced at the expense of our integrity. We need friendship and space and freedom to be just who we are, growing in our own way at our own pace. We need to be loved, to have a sense that there is a loving power greater than ourselves who, while preserving our free will, works furiously behind the scenes to pull every string possible to make our lives a thing of beauty. A power who tells us every waking second if we but listen that we are as welcome in the garden as the first blossoms of spring. At the risk of sounding sacrilegious, we need to know there is a God willing to be stupidly extravagant on our behalf. And so God is.

If ever there need be proof that God has a sense of humor, all we have to do is remember the unexpected, sometimes bizarre, certainly unpredictable ways and times that God has chosen to send us a message. Once the mind is pried open, a God-touch or God-blast (whichever seems most needed at the moment) can come from almost anywhere. Even the ridiculously secular can become a temple of the sacred.

Always the community is a base of communication. As the branch cannot survive without the tree, so spiritual growth cannot safely flourish outside of the community. When Christ took the bread and wine commanding that we "do this in memory of me," that is what was meant. A meaning must be shared, nurtured, encouraged, coaxed into the light if it is to prosper. Community must be where it is safe to be, safe to share our stories, safe to reveal our deepest needs, and within the limits of the resources of the community, find those needs met. Christian community is where those who have met the stranger on their way to their own Emmaus, gather together and in the blessing and breaking of the bread, find they are not traveling, now or ever, alone.

Whatever else may be going on in the community, if this burning, Christ-centered life is present, people will be able to find their way home. And they will come in staggering numbers. In an age of such spiritual hunger, any community that offers the direction and tools forged in the white hot furnace of God's transforming love may well face multiple problems, but getting enough people to fill the church will not be one of them. And to that kind of community will flock—indeed have flocked—many of the recovering Catholics who seek the spiritual home that perhaps they have never known.

Gifts

Gifting one another is a skill,
it demands a way to look at one another and the world not
commonly understood.
That way is first to see the beauty that is there.
Then perhaps to see the brokenness.
To miss first of all the beauty is to see first the
wounded dents.
Those who see first of all the dents see first of all
themselves as fixers — not healers.
To be healed is to be loved.
To know you are loved is to know it is safe to be here,
to know it is safe to bloom here is to find home.

5

Ministry: In Love and It Shows

The need for a chapter on ministers is a function of simple logic. If the primary prerequisite for children of faith is first of all the meeting and greeting of the One who calls them into community—into family—how much more essential is such a meeting for the one who stands at the core of that family, the minister. (For the sake of brevity, the term *minister* will be used hereafter to denote rabbi, priest, deacon, bishop, pastor, preacher, nun, monk, religious coordinator—in other words, anyone who is ordained, is a member of a religious order, or works as a professional minister.)

We have stated that real community only springs into existence when its members encounter a living God, so surely this must hold true for the one who is called to inspire, motivate, shepherd, and ultimately to celebrate the gradual transformation of that community into the living, breathing Body of Christ. For many recovering Catholics, that description might well provoke a sudden desire to grab a can of spray paint and mentally draw bull's eyes on every priest of memory—especially on those hardhearted, inflexible, arrogant professional religious who seem to haunt so many once religious hearts.

Understandable. But even as I write these words my mind fills with images and memories of tremendously overworked, stressed out ministers doing the very best they could at what had become for many near impossible jobs. For all their faults and blindness—from which none of us is exempt—I vividly recall countless wistful comments from such overtaxed religious wishing for even a tiny bit more time to prepare homilies, but with a thousand and one meetings to attend and various other—always urgent—responsibilities, that time just couldn't be found.

For others, it was the frustrated agony of having to step into a role for which they were totally unqualified or simply detested, such as fund-raising or administration. Many a fiery young priest or nun hit a head-crushing wall upon realizing that ordination or profession of vows did nothing to provide the skills and abilities demanded by the job. Some, totally devoid of resources to deal with serious issues and the huge emotional reactions they prompted, were nevertheless thrust into those situations and were told to sink or swim. Many sank. It was terribly unfair as there was no way in the world they could have adequately performed. As any of us might do, they found ways to cope. Some hid, some withdrew, some turned deaf to their critics, some put on even heavier masks of arrogance—and thus they carried on.

I remember a most loving, gentle priest who found any kind of conflict, let alone downright street fighting, totally abhorrent. This poor soul was shipped off to take charge of a parish at war over the closing of a school. This was his first parish assignment and he was told that as pastor he was to "take care of business." The outcome of the issue is not important. What it did to him is. It crushed him. Hundreds left, deploring his inept leadership. Everyone was angry. He had been asked to be someone he was not, function with skills he lacked both by temperament and training, or pay the price. And pay he did!

On another occasion, at a priest's prayer meeting, I listened while a middle-aged pastor described to me the religious community in which he lived and was supposed to lead. One member was a viciously angry young man who always found scriptural justification for his consistently negative response to any demand the community might make on him. "You can't ask that guy to do a single thing," the frustrated pastor told me, "without ending up in a fight. He's enough to drive me crazy with all his talk about freedom and respect. Freedom and respect," he snorted, "all he cares about are his own selfish opinions."

A second member of this community was in happy retirement. More than willing to take on any kind of responsibility, he simply was not physically able to do so.

A third, and here his eyes rolled heavenward, was a nice enough man, quite willing to work, but unfortunately seemed to be borderline nuts. "He sees the Virgin Mary popping out of the statues telling him to do all sorts of wondrous and holy things."

The fourth was an alcoholic still in the throes of his disease and the fifth was brand new, fresh from ordination. "Green as grass, but truly a fine young man." He sighed deeply.

"So this is my community. Apart from the obvious problem of having a zillion things to do running a large modern parish, who am I supposed to talk to? Where is my real community?"

He had none. Worse, basically he did not trust anyone who was not ordained, so he lived his life and acted out his ministry alone, a ministry that was based upon the calling of others to a community he neither enjoyed nor had any idea how to create. He shared with no one.

Having said all this, I am very well aware that many will respond with little or no sympathy. Whatever the reason, no matter how well understood or justified, they have been deeply, seriously wounded—or worse—by clerical insensitivity. Recently, a large package of material was sent to me by a young woman seeking to start a support group for all those (and she assured me there were many) who had been sexually abused by priests and other ministers. The damage at the hands of clerics runs the gamut from this horrifying extreme to a scenario heard at the closing of a seminar last night. A young woman was moving, appropriately enough, from anger to forgiveness about a priest whose counsel she and her boyfriend had sought concerning their relationship. She was extremely hurt by her perception of the minister's failure to confront the man on his apparently abusive behavior. She was left with the feeling that the minister constantly put her down, totally insensitive to her position.

After considerable thought, she wrote him a letter expressing her feelings and requesting a meeting where they could deal with the issues face to face. Here it was, two months later, and he still had not responded. In her case, anger expressed itself in the form of deep hurt rather than outward rage. She was terribly disappointed that this man who preached such beautiful truths was apparently unwilling to meet with her in honest dialogue about this most important matter in her life. Her rather stunning comment was, "I feel so sad now that I have to leave the church."

The perception that she had to leave the church because of this unfortunate experience with the minister is one question. The central concern for this chapter however, whatever the reality of the situation cited above may be, is that professional clerics possess real power. They have enormous clout. By and large, many people still invest in the cleric the very power to speak for God. For ever so many, the cleric *is* the burning bush of God in their lives. For good or ill, the minister makes a difference for millions of people.

In any serious consideration of recovering Catholics, whether in their flight from or their return to religion and community, at some point the spotlight must inevitably fall on the professional cleric.

Some twenty years ago, Fr. Henri Nouwen wrote a marvelous book for community leaders entitled *Creative Ministry*. His agenda was to point out the danger to professional ministers of falling victim to professionalism. The premise was that ministers must be able to "go beyond" the main functions of their work in order to tap into the inner reality, the inner dynamic from which the functions sprang in the first place. Professionalism bespeaks the need for skills. "Going beyond" those skills is the realm of the spirituality of the minister. That life-changing encounter with Christ lies at the heart of the minister's spirituality. It is only from that encounter that genuine spiritual power is generated.

Nouwen does a masterful job of pointing out the trap of stopping at mere professionalism. There are other traps. Simply the conditions of the times are one. With shrinking numbers of clergy, the work load for the remainder is enough to kill a horse. The pluralism of present-day congregations makes demands that require clergy to be more public relations magician than minister. Differing viewpoints on complex issues make it more difficult than ever to establish healthy boundaries in this frightfully bewildering world.

Professionalism

The great tendency for anyone who deals with a subject or body of truth (system of belief) for a prolonged period of time is that familiarity breeds boredom if not contempt. Professionals can become so accustomed to a set prescription, a formula, a way of doing things, that the performance becomes an end unto itself. "Doing it" becomes more important than communicating the meaning underlying what is being done.

Waitpersons reciting the specials of the evening, which they have already repeated a hundred times that night alone, become almost unintelligible. The litany of towns where stops will be made on a mass transit system is often a meaningless babble.

When the focus of services concerning human beings becomes repetitious it is even more dangerous. Dentists or dental hygienists who have worked on countless teeth can easily forget there are people underneath all that enamel . . . people who feel pain!

When the subject transcends human service and becomes spiritual service, perhaps the tendency and tragedy is greater still. How easy under the burden of years of repetition—let alone the pressure of the task—to forget that the truths are about God and religion. The real task is to communicate those truths in such a way that the human recipients are most enabled to integrate those realities into their own lives.

Professionalism is a very real danger in ministry. After all, when the ministers have preached over and over on the very subject they most need to hear, it becomes doubly difficult to break through that shield of professionalism. "I've said that myself a thousand times," the response comes back. "I know all there is to know about what they are saying. I don't need to listen to that." The wall thickens.

For just this reason, Nouwen makes the point that the true minister is constantly called to "go beyond." It is not enough simply to function. The point is to go beyond the task to the deeper, more powerful, fuller meaning of ministerial calling. That deeper calling, always expressed in the "going beyond" is grounded in the most personal of all experiences, an encounter with one's God. When that experience becomes the focal point of the ministerial activity, the wall of professionalism vanishes. Only then what is being done in the name of ministry is fresh, new again, and assures that *this person, here and now, first hand*, gets as much as was given to the very first person to whom this minister ever reached out.

As real a trap as professionalism is, certainly demanding attention to that aspect, there are other traps. As already discussed, the nature of the job alone is enough to distract the minister, not to mention the nature and structure of the seminaries and schools of theology that prepare our ministers for what will be asked of them. Yet another very real trap exists as well.

If codependency is a major obstacle to the experiencing of God by an individual, and consequently becomes a major obstacle to a truly Christ-centered community, then how much more it becomes a major obstacle for the minister. Called to stand at the very heart of this Christ-centered community, beckoning, inspiring, shepherding, organizing, it is simple logic that ministers, above all, must first understand and then deal with the codependency that may be obstructing their walk with God.

Nouwen categorizes the main functions of ministry and then points out what the "going beyond" must mean if professionalism is to be bested. Basically building on those categories, let us examine what the "going beyond" means in terms of battling the codependency that may be choking off the Christ power of the minister. The six categories under consideration are: Pastoral Care or Ministry, Teaching, Preaching, Organizing, Celebrating, and Leadership. Now consider these ministerial functions alongside the six codependent traits we examined in chapter 3. It will then become clear how these codependent traits, which are obstacles to individual spirituality and to the formation of community, also become the primary obstacles to the functioning of ministerial activities.

MINISTERIAL FUNCTION		CODEPENDENT OBSTACLE
Pastoral Care—Being	vs.	Poor identity, weak boundaries
Teaching—Trust	vs.	It is not safe to be here
Preaching—Surrender	vs.	Stay in control at all times
Celebrating—Independence	vs.	Lifeless obedience
Organizing—Vision	vs.	Do not risk, settle for crumbs
Leadership—Acceptance	vs.	Inability to accept love

Pastoral Care/Ministry: Being vs. Doing

Over the decades, the concept of pastoral ministry has undergone enormous change. At the turn of the century, ministry assumed the role of the shepherd for the immigrant, possibly illiterate, newcomers. A very strong hand was needed here to protect, guide, and set down the rules. Images of such heavy-handed, albeit well-intentioned ministers are thoroughly documented in the history of those times. The job description called for a kind of benevolent dictator. Most recovering Catholics who were raised in the parochial school system have vivid recollections of the inflexible rigidity of the professional pastoral care givers—the priests and nuns who were the only ones there at that time. They could count on strict, exact answers to what constitutes sin, what would please God, and how God speaks to the human heart. And of course, there were always the collections for those poor pagan babies!

Amid all the confusion about what appropriate ministry should be in the last few decades, Fr. Kevin O'Shea, an Australian theologian, has developed a contemporary model he calls eucharistic ministry. This ministry, first of all, he explains, is not built around having the right answers, or the ultimate truth, or somehow plopping Christ down into people's lives apart from who the ministers are who are doing the plopping. He calls this eucharistic model the model of simply "being with."

The basic premise is that the major task of the pastoral minister is to be with, to be present to people in all their humanity. However trite such phrases as "in all their humanity" might be, the meaning is clear. It is a common human experience that what we most crave at times is not an answer but just someone to be there. In fact, just being there may *be* the answer. Intruding answers to unasked questions may well invalidate any help those answers could have provided.

If ministry is truly about the communication of Christ and the essence of the presence of Christ is the presence of love, then we may conclude that to communicate Christ's love is to communicate the absolute best we have and know of love. And is not the primary responsibility of love simply to *be* rather than to do? Does not love first of all ask of the lover to care enough, putting self aside, really to see the one to be loved? See—in order that this person can truly be heard and understood—by being acutely present to them. This is not abstract philosophy, nor a way to exploit through control, "pushing their buttons" to create some desired effect, but it is just for the sake of presence. To be with them. To walk with them. To share the pain, to express concern, to offer help or advice or just a shoulder to lean on.

The problem with this understanding of pastoral care, of course, is that it requires very different skills and abilities from just being a baptized ordained answer book! It takes quite a different person to attempt ministry as presence rather than salvation through correct catechism responses. Ministry as presence requires that the minister has first of all established presence with self, not just on an intellectual level but on an emotional level as well. It is a given that we cannot love others until we can love ourselves. It is equally true that being present to others cannot happen unless we have at least gained some sense of what they must be feeling or going through. It is not a requirement actually to have cancer or to be an alcoholic before being able to offer healing support to one who suffers from either of these diseases. But it is imperative that we have in some similar fashion faced our own frailties, our own mortality and shame, our own doubts and fears. Only then can we be fully present to someone else . . . in the fullness of their humanity.

CODEPENDENCY AND BEING: LOSS OF IDENTITY, WEAK BOUNDARIES

A third major pitfall, until now lightly touched upon and very little understood, is the degree to which codependency exists, its impact upon the ministers, and how it affects their ministry. Codependency is not a matter of doing this or that. It is not primarily a matter of doing at all. It is truly a matter of being. Somewhere deep inside of us there is a center where we interpret the world in which we live and move and to which we respond, and this center is the very home of codependency. The codependency of the minister becomes a fundamental issue when considering the state of the community that can only be as healthy as the spirituality of its members. They take their cue from the community leaders, who in turn interpret their role and act out their ministry according to the lights coming from their own center. Codependency has a profound effect on how bright those lights may be.

It is worth restating that these simple chapters are not meant to be an in-depth treatment of the nature, cause, or recovery from codependency. They are, however, meant to emphasize that codependency is a major concern when considering the nature of spirituality.

Teaching: Beyond Transfer of Knowledge—Trust

Real teaching, of course, is not the mere putting forth of material for students to memorize, but instead it is the ability to inspire and motivate the pupils to become involved with what they are learning. One is the outer shell, the other is the living soul within the taught material.

Memorizing historical dates is one thing. Being enthralled with the lives of real people as they flowed through past centuries is another. Reciting a theorem of mathematics pales beside the thrilling experience of the elegance of numbers—or even a brief glimpse of that beauty and elegance. Most of us can recall a teacher in our past blessed with the ability to bring the lesson plan to life. These were the people truly in love with their subjects—and it showed. Because of that love they never tired of trying to find ways to impart that same love to their students. It hardly mattered what grades the pupils got, they all came away, at the very least, knowing the teacher was truly involved. As anyone who has ever been involved with a true believer, they also came away a bit more open, a bit more inclined to see the beauty of what was being offered. And always there were those few, those inclined both by nature and this special nurture, who truly caught the flame. These are the ones who took the torch from the teacher's hand, carrying that divine inspiration to those who came after.

In the context of Christian ministry, such soul fire could hardly be more crucial. Teaching here is much larger than the content understood as a body of doctrine. In ministry, the content is the conversion. The content is a life lived so as to express the power and miracle of a life set free by the power of Christ. This teaching cannot be laid out in a lesson plan, a series of lectures, or a semester of classes. This teaching is the depth of the encounter that the teacher has had with the living Christ and the power of that living Christ in their own lives.

CODEPENDENCY AND TEACHING: IT IS NOT SAFE TO BE HERE

Standing squarely in the path of this "going beyond" in the realm of teaching is the matter of trust. Those lacking the ability to trust are simply incapable of giving witness to the peace and security of surrender, the knowing by faith and experience that God is always there to bear us up.

Trusting that those who count the Sunday collection won't steal from the offering, or that volunteers will show up in time to teach Sunday school or staff the booths of the bazaar is not the kind of trust I mean here. Rather it is the willingness and the ability to become vulnerable. It is trusting one's own humanity enough truly to know oneself. It is the kind of trust displayed by those in love with life and all that is human to the extent that, to the best of their abilities, there are no dark corners left in their lives. There are no unopened closets. That quality of trust in the human condition, especially as touched and molded by the hand of the Divine, means there is no need to hide from one's innermost self.

Those who have worked through trust issues and are truly in touch with themselves know full well what their needs and feelings are. They have faced intimacy issues and have healthily incorporated them into their lives. They have dealt honestly and fairly with love. They know their relationship with authority so that they are neither cowed by it (especially with the knowledge that Christ often flew in the face of established political power), nor do they have a deep-seated need to confront purely for the sake of confronting. Trusting that they have honestly examined their own motives and motivation, they know exactly what lies beneath their attitudes and actions.

Trusting means not only trusting one's self but others as well. Ministers easily fall prey to the mentality that says "I trust God, so other than a convenient surface alliance, I have no need to trust others." Yet a life without honest feedback is a life exposed to the ravages of delusion—it is often a life preaching trust and openness while remaining unwilling or unable to trust enough to allow others into its innermost parts. How then could we expect such a person to be capable of forming a community based on mutual trust and sharing? Such "strong" individuals may indeed attract and gather many like-minded people around them, but isolation and distancing of others are not the ingredients for a true Christian community.

Here are some valuable questions for any minister who is focusing on the issue of trust:

1. With whom do you really share?
2. With whom are you totally honest?
3. Who truly knows you—not just what you think, but what you feel, what your needs are, what your desires, fears, and doubts may be?
4. Who do you regularly invite to listen and to offer feedback on a personal as well as a professional level?

As a person who has conducted countless religious retreats and seminars over the years, more often than not the answers I heard to these pointed questions were feeble indeed. Feeble, or avoided with the aforementioned attitude—"I share with God—I need no one else."

Codependency that comes in the form of a lack of or inability to trust may express itself by hiding behind dogma or tradition or by communicating to others that either they are not safe or they are completely unimportant. Lacking this hugely important Christian virtue of trust (how can one not trust having once met and walked with God?) there remains only an attitude of arrogance, inflexibility, unwillingness to learn and change, and an insufferable patronizing stance that shouts, "My knowledge is far superior to yours, therefore do not question, just obey!"

Surely one of the greatest lessons taught by Christ was that there was no need for elaborate or desperate defenses with him. It was *safe* to be just who we were if only *we trusted* enough to drop our shields. It is the lived belief in that trust that is the hope of a transformed world. It is the lived belief in that economy that requires trust. Codependency makes trust impossible.

Preaching: Beyond Telling the Story—Surrender

Our point here is certainly not to attempt a treatise on the theology or mechanics of preaching. Rather it is simply to point out that the first purpose of all Christian ministers is to spread the Word. A most sacred manifestation of that function is the blessing and responsibility of preaching. But, as Fr. Nouwen so clearly tells us, the preaching must go beyond merely telling the story.

Recently, I had the privilege of being part of a powerful preaching event. Strangely enough, it was not in a church nor carried out by professional ministers. It was at a gathering of recovering heroin addicts and was conducted by the addicts themselves.

I know full well this may not equate with the strict definition of preaching—there was no pulpit—but it certainly suffices in the sense that the saving power of Christ was proclaimed in the lived lives of those who participated in this event.

True enough, most recovering addicts do not proclaim the name of Jesus Christ, at least not as a centerpiece of their journey to fullness. One is much more likely to hear "God as I understand God to be." But these particular addicts had encountered a singular professional, a doctor who dealt not only with their chemical addiction but also with the quality of their lives. For many, a central part of their treatment came after detoxification. It was a cleansing ceremony. The doctor believed that it was not enough simply to take away the chemicals—something must replace them. Emptying is one thing. Filling is another. After the opiates had been scrubbed from their systems, he observed how guilt, shame, and anger weighed on his patients. He realized that it was imperative to eradicate such dreadful burdens if the whole life was to be saved.

Being a vibrant Christian, he had no doubt that the saving power of Christ was needed to fill these vacated hearts. It was the presence of the person of Christ who, on the wings of the spirit, would effect the passage from death to life. So as he felt led, he met one-on-one with these newly detoxified individuals and lead them through a ritual where they envisioned the purity and power of Christ who sought to enter their lives that they might be lived to the fullest. Symbolically, the recovering addicts surrendered all the burdens they carried within, thus opening themselves to the light who is Life.

Far more often than not, the experience was profound. As the doctor said, "It worked"—not as in a scam or scheme, but the way "it" always works when a heart is opened to the power of God. Deeper than the healthy and healing release of tears, the change was real—enduring. A marvelous new building could now be built on this solid foundation. A new perception of self and what that self could become in the power of a Christ-centered community was formed. The experience in itself was not growth. Daily activity that truly creates and builds a new person was needed. But that experience was a promissory note for what could be. It cleared the decks so that the miracle could unfold unimpeded.

Rituals are just rituals, however. Like musical instruments, the music they make depends on the inspiration and skill of the person playing them. This healing man was a true believer who had had a profound experience of Christ in his own life—thus he was a clear conduit for channeling this experience to others as well. His "preaching" was not focused on the words, but rather on the Word who gave the words life.

The meeting of these recovering individuals, the light in their eyes, the love shining between them, the support and caring, the depth of their words, would do any church in America proud. If that dynamic of passing from death to life is what Christ came to effect, then what happened and is happening among those addicts is what all churches are called upon to create. At the core of every church community, as at the core of this band of glorious pilgrims, stand—must stand—those who have met their God head on and become the mountain in their midst calling down the divine fire of love.

Many times, while recounting my experiences with these addicts to more traditional clergy and church members, the rejoinder has been, "This isn't A.A.; our church people aren't recovering addicts. You are comparing apples with oranges."

I am not at all sure that such is the case. Many recovering Catholics have either fled or remained locked in apathy precisely because there was no fire from the pulpit to touch them. No words were ever directed to their "death," to all those invisible anchors so firmly tethering them from rising to a higher, more spiritual quality of life.

Preaching, no matter what form it takes, is not about telling the story, it is about *being* the story.

CODEPENDENCY AND PREACHING: STAY IN CONTROL OF EVERYTHING

As we have said, surrender means opening up, not giving up. As the addicts mentioned above discovered, surrender is the act whereby all that was held prisoner within finally finds the power and the energy to burst open the prison doors, opening the way for an indwelling of new light, new power, new perception!

Surrender is not easy. Its absence, however, is a major trademark of codependency. The more one has learned, either early in life or later on from an endless, repetitive series of actions and reactions, to pull away, to close down, to button up, to protect oneself, the more difficult it will be to operate in the realm of the freedom of Christ as opposed to the inflexibility of law. Tradition, ritual, and routine will become ends unto themselves, encased in impotence.

Those who find it difficult to surrender seem forever to be setting limits as to how God can work. They build a mental frame saying, "God is in here—anywhere else is suspect. This is how God is to be contacted. Any other way is suspect." Thus is lost the incredibly dynamic sharing of believers whose testimony gives evidence that God's ways so outdistance any boundaries set by man that they are beyond guessing.

To the degree that clergy persons are unable to surrender, their preaching is paralyzed. To the degree that they are not conduits of the improbable, they are jailers of the Word of God.

Celebration: Independence

In the context of ministry, celebration has a connotation different from its usual meaning. In popular usage, celebration means to have a party. It means to focus on frivolity, to put aside that part of life that may be sad or difficult, at least momentarily. We equate celebration with fun, and confirmed by the flood of commercials with which we are daily bombarded, fun means escape.

In the theological use of the word, celebration means the opposite. Rather than escape, celebration means to encounter, to embrace. It implies running to, not running away from. Theologically, celebration means to seek that deeper level of meaning, to relive an event that profoundly changed us. It makes perfect sense then to use the expression to "celebrate" the sacraments, to celebrate the Eucharist—the Mass. By entering each time into the ritual of these sacraments we are drawn into their inner meaning and thereby touched, changed, reinforced once again by the power and light they are meant to convey.

To celebrate in this theological sense means becoming living witnesses to what our words proclaim. The power of that witnessing depends on whether or not we ministers have stood on sacred ground in front of the burning bush and have been changed ourselves. The ministerial life becomes a proclamation that Christ makes a difference—not just because we say so but because our lives say so.

Such a fascinating question: How much difference does Christ make in our lives? Not just in words, but in attitude and actions! How much does it show? How bright a light is our witness to those around us, signaling that the difference is profound?

SECURITY

Christ proclaims that independence is inherent in those who have heard and internalized the Word that comes through no other way. Without Christ, security becomes based on mundane concerns such as finances, acceptance by others, protection from criticism or risk, the size of one's intellect, and the size of the congregation to which one ministers.

With Christ, none of these carries much weight. They are of minor importance. One who truly lives in Christ finds security rests not in one's own abilities or successes, but in a wider, deeper dimension. To live in Christ is, in a most mysterious but concrete sense, to live by a different, independent agenda. It is to live by virtue of a "secret" that there is more to what is seen, success measured beyond numbers, wisdom deeper than any knowledge. Those whose lives celebrate the difference Christ makes simply run on different tracks than those who do not.

One of my heroes is a Jesuit brother who ran a unique treatment center in a state mental hospital. His program was for the "chronics" who seemed to be constitutionally incapable of achieving and maintaining sobriety. Many of his clients, some with multiple DWI's, had tried treatment ten or twenty times. Under lock and key, they were forced into sobriety while they underwent the other aspects of their treatment. Even with this program, the percentage of on-going sobriety remained pitifully small.

I once asked him how he could live with so much failure and the expectation of failure. His reply, reflecting the difference Christ makes, was "every day these men live sober is a success. Every day they stay sober they have a crack at a better life. So I don't consider any of this failure."

Such serenity, such a beautiful light shone from his eyes that regardless of one's opinion on the modality of his program, one could not help but be moved. His whole life, as any true minister who has been touched by the divine fire, was a life lived in love, always envisioning what redeemed humanity could be, and it showed. His life was a celebration—not of the misery people can generate, but of the possibility of what they can become.

CODEPENDENCE AND CELEBRATING: LIFELESS OBEDIENCE

The process of maturation is the process of differentiating one-self from the unquestioned observance of norms and moral dictates. Maturity is taking responsibility for who one is and how one behaves based on free personal choice rather than a slavish adherence to what one "should" or "is expected" to be. Maturity is based on free choice. Codependency is immaturity. Maturity is independence. Codependency is dependence. If Christian celebrating is the process of embracing all that is human in the context of a life impregnated with the meaning of Christ, it obviously then means making one's own free decisions. It means that such a life is never based on fear, guilt, or the drive to fulfill the expectations or needs of others. The initial requirement for celebrating life is first of all to celebrate our own existence. All mature, adult existence is an expression of our having grown to the point where we know who we are and are doing what we do because of our free decision. Only from that standpoint are we able to pass beyond our own emotional obstacles truly to embrace the reality of other lives.

The difference Christ makes is far more than an intellectual treatise. It reaches far beyond all learned theology. Rather it is the inner light of one's own being, fanned to brilliance, impossible to hide, because of a decision in favor of Christ, free from or at least moving toward freedom from enslaving codependency. Only from that vantage point can the Spirit pervade the inner house of the minister, suffusing every nook and cranny. And that infusion turns the minister into a powerful celebrator of the difference Christ makes in the economy of human life.

VALIDATION

It is impossible to give oneself perspective. Insight into self requires input from others. An ancient dictum of spiritual life is that wisdom results first from the journey within and then from the journey without. Balance is achieved and subsequently maintained through the dynamic of tension between an inner life consisting of meditation, personal prayer, examination of conscience, perhaps journaling or log keeping, and a thoroughly accountable outer life. The whole point of having a spiritual director is to provide feedback and insight concerning the journey without. Perhaps more than in any other area of life this relationship is required if one is to identify the codependency lurking deep within.

It is imperative, when trying to assess these areas of ministry and their corresponding obstacles of codependency, that one acquire validation from others. A suggestion might be that, even if only temporarily, the ministers gather some trusted individuals who will give them accurate information as to how they see them carrying out the functions of their ministry. Trusted means not just to concur but trusted to tell the truth as they honestly see it. So often, ministry concerns itself with topics and issues far removed from these fundamental personal areas of codependency. Yet, as I have diligently tried to point out, it is precisely these areas of codependency that dictate the quality of one's ministry.

Invite these select, trusted people to mirror to you what they observe. Do they in fact see and sense that you go beyond the transfer of knowledge in your teaching, beyond telling the story in your preaching, beyond the skillful response in your pastoral care? Do they sense your life as a celebration of the difference that Christ makes? Do they experience you as truly present to their lives, able to relate to and understand their feelings, their loneliness, doubt or joy? Do you come across as someone who has and is experiencing your life as open to what may come, rather than tightly bound up in ritual and routine? Are you their pastor, their lightning rod of the Divine? Do they sense that you honestly strive to set them free to find God in their own way? Perhaps most of all, do they sense that you are truly joyful in your decision to be a minister, that it is a free, conscious decision on your part to be where you are, doing what you do? Is your ministry to them a witness that life can and should be lived as an adventure rather than a struggle? Do they see God in you?

This is not a call to be perfect. No one is or can be. Nor is this an exercise to generate guilt. It is an invitation to glean information from those who really know you, from those to whom you minister, about how you come across to them. How they see you may be very different from how you think they see you — or — how you see yourself.

CODEPENDENCY DOES NOT MEAN SICK

It is important to emphasize once more that "codependent" does not translate "sick." Far more accurately, it translates "human."

To some extent, every family system is flawed. There are neither perfect people nor perfect families. Even in the most loving (and certainly in the most religious) family systems, patterns or values can form which, if internalized or built upon in some extreme manner, can harden into practices that obstruct the grace of God.

Accurately understood, the question is not "who is or who is not codependent," but "to what extent has some pattern been internalized that obstructs the light of Christ? What are those obstacles? How have they become stumbling blocks?"

One of the subtlest aspects of codependency is that it becomes involuntarily habitual. Codependency is the result of learned and practiced behaviors and patterns. Whatever one practices soon becomes habit, sinking out of sight into the subconscious. This means when uncontested codependency is being acted out, it is not being done consciously. No one makes a conscious decision to act in a codependent manner in any given situation. It simply has become natural and normal, as the way we breathe or fold the morning paper or brush our teeth. It becomes who we are.

As with all habits, once set in motion by repeated action, they quickly set up systems that support, protect, and reinforce their power. Habits being what they are, ministers will naturally gather around them those people who fit into their manner of operation, no matter how codependent that may be. Of course, to them it doesn't feel codependent, it feels normal. Being normal, they will defend its right to rule with all their might and mane. Opinions or criticisms that challenge what has become "normal" are easily pushed aside as reactionary, ignorant, or unimportant. Situations where such opinions or criticisms might be encountered are studiously avoided. People offering such opinions are simply laughed at or otherwise discredited. More often than not, they are categorized as trouble-makers.

Trouble they may be, yet what they are saying can be very important. No matter the manner in which they voice their opinions, or how valid their motives, *what* they are saying may be pointing directly at the minister's codependency.

Who Do You Say That I Am?

A benchmark in the development of the disciples came when Jesus asked Peter, "Who do you say that I am?" The question was not asked on a theoretical, intellectual plane. Jesus was asking Peter to go deep within himself and answer from his heart. Basically, it was the same question Moses asked of God in the burning bush, "Who shall I say sent me?" In both cases, whether in the Old or New Testament, how, and from what depth that question is answered, will dictate the power of the ministry. We have recognized that the power of any minister depends, at least humanly speaking, on whether that minister has encountered the Word, not just through the intellect but in the very core of being. We know now, more than was ever imagined, the depth which that encounter can plumb depends upon the degree of the minister's freedom from codependency. Codependency is rooted in the subconscious level of every living human being, most often unseen and therefore unchallenged. Its presence more than likely needs the input of others in order to be clearly identified. The remedy for and healing of its presence certainly needs enormous courage and humility. Yet it is the very healing of that spiritual cancer that enables the love that is within to shine forth in all its power and glory.

Organizing: Beyond Structure—Vision

Organizing takes its direction from the purpose the organization has been formed to serve. Whether the Girl Scouts, a motorcycle gang, or a national government, the development of organization will always reflect the purpose and vitality of the ideal it is meant to promote.

The trouble with organization and structure, of course, is that they easily become ends unto themselves. They set up like concrete, soon existing only to serve themselves; they are like some poor prehistoric beast stuck in a tar pit that sucked it dry of life. The eternal task of structures, necessary whenever people gather together to accomplish a goal, is to keep them from swallowing up the ideal they were formed to serve.

The primary question then for organizations and structures of Christian community is: What is the purpose of this community and how brightly does its light shine? Once the purpose is lost or allowed to drift toward or be kidnapped by the most powerful person in that community, the center starts to unravel. A community minus its purpose is a dangerous loose cannon. Purpose demands organization. The question then is: What *in fact* is the purpose of the individual community, not as outlined in a well-crafted mission statement, but in fact. Where does the energy go; what are the actual priorities; what in fact is happening? How much of the open-armed, loving Christ is in evidence? Is change evident? Are people's lives transformed? Do faces shine? Is there a joy and energy about the place that bespeaks a group of folks who have tasted the power of life over death and are growing in the sharing of that wondrous story? Does the structure of the community, rather than militate against such a display of Christ-power, actually help to make it a reality?

There is a lovely bridge in the city where I live, called "Irene's bridge." It spans sixteen lanes of traffic and leads from a busy section of downtown to a restful park and art center. The bridge was built by Irene's loving husband as a memorial to her after her death.

He told me Irene always loved the symbolism of a bridge — getting people together, crossing over differences and obstacles, meeting in the middle. She was a mover and shaker in the business part of town, but she also loved art and that serene park. She longed to share her experience as any lover of beauty loves to share it with others. That noisy, bullying sixteen lanes of traffic became a constant irritant to her. It got in the way.

As she lay dying, her husband told her he was going to build a bridge across all that chaos in her name — to honor her spirit — so anyone who so desired could easily cross over into that peaceful place of rest and refreshment. And thus a mighty steel bridge came into being. The purpose dictates the organization. That which is on the inside will manifest itself in concrete expressions.

Is Christ available in the Christian communities? Does the institution support the kinds of causes and activities that crack the cold, hardened faces and hearts so often encountered, letting the radiant, pulsing, caring face of Christ shine through? Is there room for me who may be different, or hurting? Hurting so badly that in my pain I put barriers between us, because I am so afraid that if I let you in, you will reject me. Will you be there for me long enough, strong enough that my fear will not be stronger than your love?

There are countless ways organization either kills the spirit or liberates it that it might more fully transform the world.

At the core of the community stands the leader. At the core of the leader stands the power generated by the experience of having laid hands on the heart of God.

CODEPENDENCY AND ORGANIZING:
DO NOT RISK, SETTLE FOR CRUMBS

The line between rhetoric and reality can be as thin as a sun-beam or as wide as the ocean. Rhetoric is the easy part. It is not difficult to spin fine words. Those words have substance only as deep as the person speaking them.

By far the hardest part of following Christ is to surrender to belief in the vision offered by Jesus. In so many ways, both rooted in our personal history and the demands of our present stack of problems, the vision can be lost. Or never claimed. Only too soon, life teaches us to settle for the lowest common denominator as our vision of life. "It is hard; no one gets ahead; don't expect too much; you are on your own; it won't work anyway; and besides, what will the neighbors say?" Add those thoughts to all the little daily crises, and it is no wonder living a vision of reality that says it *can* work, you are *not alone*, we *can* do all things, and who *cares* what the neigh-bors say, is so often missed. How easy to put the energy and attention necessary to grasp and claim this vision in that pile of calls to be made when time allows. Of course, time never allows. Until striving to claim that vision, or finding time to make it a central part of life becomes a top priority, it will never happen.

My lovely old catechetics professor often stated that the only question Christ would ask of his ministers would be, "Will people be able to find me there?" By "there" he meant the communities we were to establish and from which we would be teaching. The answer to that question depends, to a large extent, on how much of the codependent mud the minister has cleaned off the windows of the soul in order to grasp and glory in that vision given to us by Christ.

Leadership: On Fire with Acceptance

Charisma can be a most frustrating word. For one thing it is elusive. For another, it seems to be classified as an inborn trait that one either has or not. To be in a profession that calls for charisma when one seems to have been born with a deficit of that commodity can be irritating beyond bearing. The hard fact is that not everyone is charismatic—whatever that means.

Elusive or not, charisma is real. Leadership is real. Movements and communities need someone to stand tall, someone who makes things happen. Leaders energize people to do more than they ever thought they possibly could. Mediocre teams can miraculously turn into world beaters when a leader comes into their midst. The difference? A leader who acted as the catalyst for belief. And belief became the wings that lifted the mundane to the extraordinary.

But how can anyone demand of, or put down, a leader—in this case the minister—who may very well have been born without these traits. Are not some people simply born dull? Criticizing them for lack of charisma is as unfair as criticizing or blaming them for how tall they are or the color of their eyes.

I think it is not the same.

No matter what part of charisma is inborn and therefore something one cannot learn, the fact remains that anyone who truly accepts and believes becomes magnetic. In different ways perhaps, but never dull. Looking into eyes that shine with excitement, it is impossible not to feel the power. The more one is touched by experiencing what one believes, wrapped in that all-encompassing, accepting love, the more potent that experience becomes and the less need there is for props and organizations to communicate that meaning. What comes from the heart touches the heart.

Charisma is 90 percent belief. Belief is 90 percent the experience of having been touched by and become part of the object of that belief. In that experience the object becomes the subject. It is no longer a matter of "it out there" but of "me changed in here."

A seminary classmate of mine was a well-loved, humorous young man but in no way a leader. He took no stands, made no ripples, and tried very hard not to rock any boats. He tried to give the right answers, keep the rules, and not be a bother to anyone. He functioned very well. Many years later, while channel hopping on television one night, I caught a program featuring this very same but now not so young man. He had spent most of his life as a priest in Brazil and had become a passionate defender of the rain forest and its people. He had been there. He had witnessed firsthand the destruction of this wonder of the world, had seen the devastation it created among his people. He was there. He was touched. He took it personally. Now he was on fire.

Perhaps that is what charisma mostly is—taking it personally. When it becomes personal, it becomes real. Then—look out. Look out or the leader may capture you in his or her net.

So it is with Christian leadership. To have it become personal, one must personally have encountered Christ. Lazarus took it personally when he was called from his tomb. The woman taken in adultery took it personally when Jesus shielded her from the stoning. The man healed on the Sabbath took it personally when all of a sudden his legs filled with strength and he could walk. Perhaps it is so with charisma—it happens when we take personally the vision given us through direct personal contact with Christ. Perhaps it is something like picking up that live electric power line blown down in a storm. Pick it up and you most surely will be changed!

Once touched by that power, the ministers no longer act to be correct, or politically right, or to be liked. Nor do they act to be different. They act the way they do because the power of the loving, accepting Christ within compels them to. Their action has a purpose and a focus—to invite all who would to become miracle-minded, to pass from death to life, to "come join us where the telling of your story is not only safe but encouraged." And in the telling of that story you will come to see infinitely more clearly, not only how powerful God is in your life, but also how beautiful you are in partnership with your Partner. With us you have found acceptance—you have found a home.

In a world dying from loneliness and alienation, what a glorious mission. In a world devouring itself in its own anger and rage, what a restless joy it is to recognize that Christian community is the answer. And at the heart of that community stands the lightning rod, the minister called to call others to their place in this ring of fire.

CODEPENDENCY AND LEADERSHIP:
INABILITY TO ACCEPT THAT WE ARE LOVED

Codependency prevents one from passing over and through doing to the deeper realm of being. Imprisoned in the need to be correct or liked or secure, or to avoid conflict or responsibility—all aspects of codependency—codependents act only to fill their own needs. Some have called this codependent self the pseudo self. Not the real self, not the real being aching to break free and assert its own truth, but a crippled and hobbled way of acting in order to protect some hoary old negative pattern learned long ago.

The more we free ourselves from such imprisonment, the more charismatic we are free to become. The less need we have to be accepted by others, the more freed up we are to be concerned with being liked and accepted by our own selves. The less need we have to be legally and politically correct, the more we are able to be humanly right. The less we need to do the will of others for some paltry reward, the more freed up we are to do the will of God, even if that puts us at odds with some powerful backers.

The pseudo self seeks security in being liked and accepted by others. The real self seeks security by never losing touch with that inner voice that leads the way home, which is back to the garden and to the One who waits for us there.

Someone whose experience of Christ has not been twisted into grotesque shapes, reflecting all those levels of the codependent pseudo self, is a work of art. When Christ and the real self link hands, beauty becomes depth and the depth of such beauty has no end. Such a person can be loving without being passive, staunch in belief without being judgmental, wise without being arrogant, realistic without being unkind, forgiving without being stupid. Being touched by Christ is not like acquiring a label—such as "Christian"—whether Catholic or Protestant. Fundamentally it is being changed—bettered. It is from that fundamental level of change that one's true being explodes and charisma is born.

Hidden Realms

So many "people" walk in our blood,
look out of our eyes from some hidden realm within.
A frequent visitor to the window of our eyes,
for anyone who will look, is the lost child.
The child who is lost is that part of us we hide,
protect, hope no one sees—
it is the "us" locked within the frozen arms of horrid
experiences long past but not gone.
The child yearning to be free enough to say I love you,
or I need you,
or please get off my foot,
free enough to say "stop,"
or "don't laugh at me,"
free enough to wrap its arms around loved ones
and love them.

6

Learning to Walk with God

This book has been a veritable catalog of obstacles to walking with God in the cool of the evening. Heading the list has been codependency. After all, it often is codependency that underlies our refusing to forgive, living in the past, carrying resentments, pitying our selves, and finding all manner of ways to cut off our noses to spite our spiritual faces. It only makes sense then to complete these pages with concrete suggestions for healing. All of these proposals, to some degree or another, are helpful in countering the effects of codependency, although this short treatment of codependency is neither detailed nor thorough. In addition to these suggestions, the reader, motivated by relating to some aspect of the codependency touched upon in these pages, may find it valuable to seek specific, directed help from a codependency specialist. Sooner or later, however, the issue of feelings will present itself, charged with obstacles to a healthier spirituality, whether or not it is called codependency.

Dealing with Feelings

Knowing that something is true while being unable to act on it with any real conviction is an experience painfully familiar to most of us. In this healing from painful religious experiences, if all we had to do was to "know better" we could expect almost instant release. Unfortunately knowledge and insight, although tremendously important aspects of growth, do not in and of themselves produce change. The main obstacle to putting such information into action is—quite simply—feelings. Those old emotions keep us from feeling good when we try to change behavior patterns or implement the new truths we may have discovered.

It is critically important to identify specifically the feelings under discussion. Where do they come from? Rather than pile them into one big spaghetti-like tangle, let us pull them apart strand by strand so we can see what they are really wrapped around and learn how to deal with them.

For example, those who had such damaging, God-obstructing religious experiences may know, as surely as they know two and two are four, that those professional ministers for whom they have such huge resentments were just people, probably doing the best they could. They may know those stern, petty nuns who so humiliated them were possibly suffering from P.M.S., a condition about which they had no knowledge. They may know that nuns of the old school were not even allowed to think that they had bodies, let alone that their bodies could have anything to do with the way they acted. They may know that those perplexed ladies may have suffered intense guilt about their behavior, going to confession over and over, yet rage and anger may still cling like a second skin. It may be perfectly clear, but there they are, stuck in that old shame and fury.

Or even if we truly believe that God loves us, we still can't seem to shake off our fear. We may reflect on the many beautiful passages in Scripture where Jesus shows his great loving care and forgiveness, we may pray and be convinced that God only desires our happiness. Our feelings, however, stubbornly remain those of anxiety, hooked perhaps to a memory in childhood when we uttered "damn" or some other such forbidden word, sure that God, the stern parent, would be obliged to punish us. So we wind up, especially if we are an identified, recognized Adult Child of a dysfunctional family, with all kinds of ways to sabotage any joyous celebration. God may want us to rejoice, but we stay mired down in feelings of guilt, shame, worry, and fear. What in the world do we do about those feelings?

First we stop and identify exactly where we are stuck, regardless of what we know. Is it anger around those professionals in our past—priests, nuns, other religious professionals? Is it rage at what we were taught in the eighth grade? Is it the guilt laid on us when we were told that if we ever missed Sunday Mass we were automatically consigned to hell? Does that guilt still plague us today, even though we know God isn't going to hurl us into the fiery furnace if we don't get to church some Sunday? The more we are willing to ponder these things, to write them down and process them, the more helpful they will be to us. Then we will be ready to take practical steps to heal those old feelings.

Six Steps to Wholeness

1. FEELINGS ALWAYS FOLLOW ACTIONS

Feelings face backward. The only thing feelings know is what was. Understand that when we are experiencing some uncomfortable feelings, they are not necessarily dealing with today's situation at all. They are simply facing backward. Feelings are learned. They are practiced. What we practice, we become. Now, suppose we are thirty, forty, fifty or more years old, and we are still experiencing all this shame and guilt, rage and fear. Perhaps we are longing to go to Communion but we can't because of a divorce or a second marriage. Perhaps our sister's or daughter's wedding is coming up, and we are unable to tolerate even entering a church. What is the root cause of those feelings? Chances are they trace back to some catechism class where those very large people in black, God's personal representatives, taught us that God was always angry with us! As adults, we are still terrified but now we are also angry! We learn, we practice, we become what we practice.

Feelings that face backward feed on yesterday's truth. We must learn in a conscious, grown-up way to discern whether we are dealing with yesterday or with today. Regardless of the way we feel, we need to act in a healthy, responsible adult manner. As we continue to act in that healthy, responsible adult manner, new appropriate feelings will follow. Those terrible feelings of guilt will diminish and, we can look upon the face of God and not experience that crippling fear. We can even learn to push the grass aside and lay our finger on the heart of God. We can learn that God indeed does love us. We can learn that. But not if we allow old feelings to lock us into the past.

Where do feelings come from? Feelings are generated by the interaction of values with behavior. When values and behavior rub up against one another they either create harmony or friction. When our behavior is in conflict with our values, feelings of guilt, fear, shame, or rage are generated, sometimes quite appropriately. If our value says "be honest" and our behavior is to lie or steal, then the feeling of guilt is entirely in keeping with our standards. What must change in order to deal with that feeling is our behavior. But when it comes to religion, so often what is out of kilter is not the behavior but the value. Until we learn to understand and process this, we tend to try to deal with the behavior when that is not the problem. We need to rummage around and pull out the value involved. Only then can we make a decision to let this value stay at the helm of our ship or replace it with a more appropriate one.

This exercise has proven to be helpful to determine conflicting values and behaviors. On one side of a piece of paper, put down the heading "Value" and on the other side, mark a column "Behavior." Now let's review some of those very common "religious values" we have looked at in previous chapters. We shall quickly see where feelings come from when values and behavior clash.

Under the "Value" heading, for instance, write down "God is only pleased with me when I am perfect." How many of us learned that! Certainly we heard the words that God loves and forgives us, but emotionally we suspected that God was really only happy with us when we were perfect. If that is the value, what is going to happen when we make a mistake, lose our temper, rage, take God's name in vain, become a little reckless with the truth, or just plain sin?

Our value is that God loves us only when we are perfect, right?

So we weren't perfect. Now when we think about God, how are we going to feel? Right! We are going to feel unworthy. We might even feel that God is outraged, just waiting to get even with us.

Take another look at that value. Do we really believe that God is only happy with us when we are perfect? One way to imagine God is as a perfect parent. It may be difficult to relate to the perfect part, but many of us can relate to the parent. Do we only love our children when they are perfect? Of course not, we say. Kids aren't perfect, people aren't perfect. We truly love our children whether they are perfect or not. Of course, when they are "being good" and performing well, we might find them more attractive, but that has nothing to do with how much we love them. We always love them no matter what. Now, looking again at God, looking again at that value, does God really only love us when we are perfect? Check the behavior that crashed into the value. How did it make us feel?

Once we understand that feelings are rooted in values, when the sensation of guilt, fear, or anger rises up, we then have the option to examine those values very carefully and vote on them! We can say "No, that is crazy stuff, and I am not going to let feelings generated from craziness run my life!"

Another belief—God inexorably punishes inappropriate behavior. Hard as it is to admit, many of us do believe that. We may try to bargain with God, try to make up for what we have done, anything to get back in God's good graces again. Perhaps we missed Mass on Sunday and our value says that we have now committed a grave sin. Monday we get up at 4:00 in the morning to start on a greatly anticipated vacation. With that value, what can we expect to happen to us on that trip? Inevitably, there will be a car wreck, or the car will be broken into, we will be mugged, lose all our money, and—we will deserve it. All the fun of the vacation will be eaten up by worry and hesitation, waiting for the other shoe to drop. God will surely punish us for missing Mass!

Until we stop and reflect, until we really pull those truths out and examine them, we have no idea what we really believe. Only when we run it through the process—value, behavior, feelings—can we make a choice about the value. This doesn't mean that we don't make a genuinely responsible effort to get to church on Sundays. But if we don't make it, regardless of the reason, to worry that God is out to get us becomes a wretched obstacle to the love of God. It ruins life.

How about "religion comes straight from God." Many people are convinced that what their religion says is perfect, immutable, to be obeyed at all times. Now, if that is our belief, but our actions disavow it, perhaps around the issue of birth control, nuclear disarmament, or women's rights, there is no way we can avoid feeling guilty and fearful when our "perfect" religion has told us that if we put any of those ideas into practice, not only will God be displeased with us but also God will inflict terrible punishment upon us. What is the value?

Long cherished is the presumption that blind obedience of the rules leads to salvation. Jesus quarreled with the Pharisees over this issue some two thousand years ago. Many people do not live a life of prayer and meditation or go to church just for the innate value of it, they do it as a sort of insurance policy against the day they die, to stay out of hell.

Blind obedience of the rules does not necessarily lead to salvation. Living our life in accordance with our conscience leads to salvation. Our conscience is not a feeling. Our conscience is our decision-making ability. Until we do the kind of work we are suggesting here, however, we really can't know what we believe. When we put our minds to it, few of us believe that blind, unthinking, mechanical observance of the rules will lead to salvation. If that is what we have been doing, we may have felt a great deal of complacency, but it becomes a dangerously dead walk.

Perhaps our value has been that others have the right to tell us who God is, what God wants of us, when God is pleased with us. Then one day we begin to think on our own. What else could we feel but guilt? Is our behavior wrong? Is it wrong to think our own truths? Is it wrong to act on those truths? Or is the value wrong? What kind of value is it that says that other people could possibly know more about who God is to us than we ourselves know?

Bordering on superstition is the value that if we "obey" and are faithful, no harm will befall us. Surely God takes care of God's own so if we go to church, put money in the basket, pray umpteen rosaries, and do all sorts of other religious things, we will be protected from sickness, loss of jobs, or any other disaster. Now, suppose some evil thing befalls us—how can we feel anything but rage?

Whenever there is emotional distress, look at the underlying value. Belief in God does not protect us from pain and misfortune. Heresy? Take a look at Jesus on the cross. He wasn't saved from pain and hurt, difficult decisions, or public disgrace. God has promised that belief in God would give us the strength and ability to deal with whatever happens to us in life. When we are connected to that power, we can pass from death to life, not just physically, or at the end of our days, but in the thousand and one minor daily crises that can promote death rather than life.

Other values around religion are "religion can't change; professional religious are above reproach." Check this out again. When we elevate ordinary people just like us into a position of special holiness, we will surely end up full of hurt and pain. We are all called to holiness. Through schooling and training, perhaps such people may have special insight, more time to pray and meditate, but be above reproach? Absolutely not. They make mistakes, they sin, they are codependent. They have character defects just like the rest of us. It is hardly fair to them to put them on such pedestals. We end up confused and hurt, wanting to tell them "what you did was wrong, it was a terrible thing to do," when our value tells us that they are above reproach, and we have no right to tell them anything. What uncomfortable feelings this belief is going to generate! Look again at the value.

It is imperative to understand that feelings most often are indicators of what we learned yesterday. What we learned may indeed be true. If that is the case, fine. We own it as true. But suppose we no longer believe those truths we learned yesterday. Like clothes worn beyond repair, we need to throw them out. Whenever our feelings swirl around religion, marrying a non-Catholic, a second marriage, divorce, or just the fact of being a woman, whatever the issue may be, we need to pull the feelings up into the conscious mind and ask, what is the value here? What is the old truth to which we are reacting? Uncovering the source of feelings is essential, especially because they have seemed so mysteriously elusive. Now we are ready to move on to the next step.

2. Accept the Feelings, Do Not Run Away from Them

We admit that whatever we are feeling is how we feel. Let us name the feelings—guilt, anger, fear, rage, shame, and yes, even that we are mad at God. We must accept, own, and call them what they are. There is a great tendency today, much in vogue, to seek instant gratification at all costs. Rather than deal with the cause of a headache, most of us are inclined to take enough aspirin to override the pain that may be sending us an important message. The same may be true when painful emotions strike.

Our tendency is to run. Rather than accept what we are feeling and find the source of the discomfort, some of us may run away from this opportunity to learn and into some form of compulsive behavior. Compulsive behavior is any activity we do to keep from feeling. It may be, for those so genetically inclined, abusing alcohol or drugs, it may be by overeating, immersing ourselves in work, getting lost in television, over-volunteering, engaging in harmful sex, and even making a compulsion of religion. It is not the activity that is the problem, it is the reason behind the activity that needs tending to.

Rather than simply accepting how we feel and learn, another form of avoidance is "shoulding" ourselves ("should" as learned in God only knows what codependent environments), discounting how we do feel in favor of how we should feel. Let us stop "shoulding" ourselves. "I should feel loving all the time." "I should not feel rage about this." "Shoulding" ourselves is an exercise in futility. Feelings are most in control of us when we are running away from them. So whatever feelings we are contending with at the moment, whether they concern going to Communion again now that we are "out of the church," or the fear of praying to a God we feel is angry with us, we stop running away. We turn around, face them, and call them what they are. This is critical if we are to attain emotional health.

3. Embrace the Feelings

It is one thing to accept the fact that we are angry, or that shame is at it again. But it is an entirely different case to embrace those feelings! When we begin to operate on the internal forum, perhaps we are not going to have the sanction of the external forum—a priest for instance—giving us permission to do what we need to do for ourselves. We may not have that blessing, we may not be told that we are loved by God, that what we are doing is fine. When we then go to the internal forum, we may feel terribly guilty. We may be so stressed that we can't do those things we need to do in order to continue our journey into healthy spirituality.

Suppose we are still churched, but some happening in our lives, that divorce or second marriage, for example, has kept us from going to Communion. Internal forum says go, but we are so paralyzed by a sensation of guilt that we are incapable of standing up and walking to the altar. Or suppose we have acknowledged the feeling. Now we must embrace it—truly feel it—grab hold of it and say, in effect, "Feelings, do your worst!"

Feelings are not the enemy! Feelings are neither good nor bad, moral nor immoral. They simply are. Feelings know nothing. Remember, they only face backward. When we own the feelings, embrace them, tell them to do their worst, much of their power over our lives dissipates. It evaporates and fades away.

An outstanding example comes to mind. One of the great psychologists of our time, Rollo May, portrays psychological exorcism—driving out demons—in his book, *Love and Will*. Dr. May learned, while visiting a primitive tribe, that their land had been occupied by the British, causing many of the natives to develop incredible fear and hatred of the conquerors. He then describes the ceremony where one of the men was to be exorcised of these terrible emotions. With the loving community seated in a circle, this man was made to put on the hated British uniform and dance around within that circle of support, ritualizing his rage and anger. He became the enemy. By embodying them, he was freed of those shackling feelings.

Internalize feelings, embrace them, walk with them. If we have a terrible fear of missing Mass, then stay home—miss Mass. If our value says that God is so angry with us that he can hardly wait to pounce on us when we die, and we are too fearful to pray, then we embrace that. Put it on! Walk with it! Become fear! We soon discover that it isn't going to kill us! There is a great deal of difference between stuffing feelings and letting go. Stuffing means burying that fear, shame, or guilt alive. Letting go means we have dealt with that emotion. Dealing with it means to understand the origin of the feeling, accept the feeling, embrace the feeling. We run out to the battlefield, take hold of the guilt we can hardly stand, lock our arms around it, and wrestle with it. Only then have we the power to let it go because it no longer owns us.

4. MAKE DECISIONS ABOUT THOSE FEELINGS

Until we have brought to a conscious level that which we are making a decision about, there is no way to make a responsible decision. We simply continue to act on a feeling without discerning its origin. We can recognize anger or anxiety, guilt or worry, but now we must go beyond just feeling it and examine the cause. What is the behavior rubbing against, what obscured belief, that generates these uncomfortable emotions? Brought into conscious awareness, we have much more accurate data with which to make our decision.

Next, we scrutinize the value itself, searching for its beginnings. Frequently, some Family of Origin work will reveal the source. Perhaps a memory will pop up of being humiliated by an old parish priest when we made a mistake while reciting our Latin. To be sure, that particular priest may have been dead for twenty years, but we are still dragging the shame around and allowing it to control the way we feel about religion. If we have equated religion and spirituality, it cannot help but dictate the quality of our walk with God.

Continuing the process, once more we examine the value to determine whether or not we still accept it as truth. We have already discussed all kinds of neurotic and unhealthy "truths," such as "God only cares for me when I am perfect." Ridiculous even to think it now, isn't it? Still, we must check it out. What behavior do we allow to be dictated by these old feelings? Do we generally allow our feelings to decide the way we are going to act? Are we afraid to remarry or even go on a vacation because God is going to ruin everything for us one way or another? So we don't go on vacation or we don't pursue a relationship that might be richly rewarding and fulfilling, adding the wonder of love and intimacy to our life. At least intellectually, most of us believe that God is love and that God wants us to have love, peace, and serenity. Does it make sense then, in the name of God, to deny ourselves the very things that could bring real joy into our life?

When we examine the value that we have allowed to dictate and control our behavior, we realize we just don't believe it anymore. When first we consult our internal forum, we may quiver and quake, sure that we will be turned into frogs for being so presumptuous as to rely on our own conscience. But when we look down, lo and behold, our feet are not webbed! We are not all green and lumpy! We have discovered that we can be in control of our feelings! This does not mean that we become "feelingless," so rigid we lose our spontaneity and enthusiasm. It simply means that when we get into an emotional bind our feelings no longer dictate how we are going to act. We make the decisions about our actions.

5. Turn Those Decisions into Action.

Feelings follow actions. It should be obvious by now that if we want to change the way we feel we must change the way we act, and although it doesn't happen overnight, we keep at it until it feels normal. Feelings know nothing. Feelings only face backward.

Here is another kind of exercise. Make two columns on your paper with these headings: "Stop Doing" and "Start Doing." We are going to make a short list of behaviors that we are going to stop doing and behaviors we will start doing. This isn't just behavior modification. We are lining up behaviors, based on our new understanding about old values and old feelings, so we can more clearly decide our future actions.

Just as we have physical muscles that we can see, let us imagine that our mental, emotional, and spiritual muscles are visible. Every time we lift weights, our muscles bulge and get stronger. Every time we act in a self-defeating way, we lift an emotional weight that develops and strengthens hurtful feelings, deepens and reinforces negative patterns. For example, we can stop endlessly justifying our behavior, stop explaining to everyone why we are divorced or justifying why we don't go to church anymore. If we understand it, if we accept the consequences, then it is our decision, and we do not need to justify it to anyone else. We can refrain from making alibis for everything that goes wrong in our life. Perhaps we still believe that because we committed some dastardly sin in the past God is taking revenge on us. God isn't doing it—we are. If deep down we still believe terrible things are going to happen to us, that we deserve to be punished, we will always find ways to sabotage our happiness and success. But it won't be God doing it! With some thought, no doubt we can add many other behaviors to our stop list.

On the start list, here are some examples from what other people have said worked for them. Pray. We don't have to be in church to pray. We can stop right now and sit quietly, opening our hearts and minds to God and listen, making conscious contact with God as we understand God to be. We can return to the sacraments. We may be saying in some distress, no, we can't do that. Who says we can't? What keeps us from doing that? Embrace those feelings. Check the internal forum. Perhaps that is exactly what we need to do. Or maybe we simply need to return to church. Any church. If we can't stand going to a church service, we go when the church is empty and quietly sit there. Do we become nauseated? Probably not. Do we recall only the bad things that happened to us in religion? Perhaps. But suppose we sit there until we recall some of the good things. It's time to decide what we are going to do in our lives right now. We know what was, but what about now?

An item on our start list might be to consider dating again or getting to know someone better who already seems quite special.

Fear may have prevented us from thinking that we could allow ourselves to get married again because of some legal restrictions of the church. Consult the internal forum before making any such decision!

Start to read the New Testament, get into Scripture. We may have thought it was too difficult, that we could never understand it. But when we quietly start to read, one of the parables perhaps, we can ask what is God saying to us in this story? Not what Father Jones or Father Smith says it means, but what does it mean to us? We can add many more items to our start list.

6. Keep Doing Healthy Behavior

This is an absolute must. Once we decide what it is that we need to do, we have to keep at it. We can't do it once and say "Thank God I whipped that one, I don't need to do that anymore." One time does not a habit break! Feelings follow actions, and like weight lifters, we must repeat the new behavior again and again until it feels as normal and comfortable as our old actions used to feel.

I'd like to share another of my favorite poems with you, "The Present Crisis" by James Russell Lowell. Mr. Lowell died in 1891 so the poem is more than a century old. I am not sure what he had on his mind when he wrote it, but it certainly applies to us in this age. He is speaking of the courage to live in the present, not allowing yesterday's truths, yesterday's experiences so to control and isolate us that we fail to live in the now. The last stanza of this rather long poem goes like this:

> New occasions teach new duties.
> Time makes ancient good uncouth.
> We must upwards still and onward
> Who would keep abreast of truth.
> Before us gleams her campfires.
> We ourselves must Pilgrims be.
> We must launch our own Mayflower.
> And steer boldly through the desperate winter sea.
> Nor attempt the future's portal
> With the past's blood rusted key.

What a powerful, contemporary message! We ourselves must steer boldly through the desperate winter sea, nor attempt the future's gate with yesterday's blood rusted key. Today is ours. We must make the decision about the quality of our life and steer resolutely into the future!

Developing a Program of Positive Spirituality

After all our discussions about understanding the role feelings play, trapping us in outdated religious values, giving our power away to the external forum, being afraid or unable to take charge of our own power, the question remains, where do we go from here? Are there practical steps we can take that will deepen our spirituality? Can we truly push the grass aside, as Edna St. Vincent Millay wrote so beautifully in her poem, and discern the heart of God in our hearts?

I am going to suggest some spiritual steps that are helpful to all of us in our pursuit of a powerful spirituality. Perfectionists, resist the temptation to think this means that each must be faithfully performed! Take what is useful and helpful and disregard the rest. These are suggestions, not rules!

There are also some other very important areas we need to take into account. If our bodies are indeed a temple of the Holy Spirit, we must take healthful nutrition and adequate exercise seriously. Many times we have heard that until these crucial points were attended to, all the spiritual steps in the world produced no results. Couch potatoes stuffing down junk food just don't seem to get up much energy to put into spiritual matters! Today, we know junk food contributes to depression, mood swings, and inertia.

Use these suggestions as springboards. Make them work for you with your own additions or subtractions.

1. TAKE TIME DAILY

We must discipline ourselves to take some time every day. Time to do what? Well, first of all, just to take some time. Many of us are so afflicted by the "hurry up" disease that we keep absolutely masochistic schedules, running from morning to night to perform thousands of tasks that, of course, simply must be done! Most of us have full-time jobs besides parenting, working on the house, and volunteering for community work. There is no time left to sit and reflect, to evaluate happenings, positive or negative, to sort out what is really going on here, especially in our church lives. For instance, what is good liturgy? For that matter, what is bad liturgy? Do we just quit going to church because we did not have a positive liturgical experience? It takes time to reflect, to think out our options.

If we can't find the time to reflect, to listen, we may know a lot of things, but we won't know what we know. Knowing something is one thing. Reflecting on it so that we know that we know, is a whole other matter. And that takes time. In prayer most of us talk to God. Meditation is for listening. To turn prayer and meditation time into yet another activity is to miss the point entirely. Only when we quiet ourselves can we hear what God is saying to us. How can we ever know where God would lead us if we never listen?

Of course, you say. Yes, indeed. We all need some quiet time. Now the question is, when exactly is that going to be? For the modern-day American, afflicted by the "hurry up" syndrome, over-committed, weighed down with anxiety unless constantly busy, until that serenity time is set in concrete, it will never happen. Suffering from mountains of guilt stemming from bad religious training, many of us don't want to be quiet. Shame-based and apprehensive, when we are quiet all we hear is ourselves, berating, belittling, putting ourselves down. Who wants to face such a torrent of self-abuse?

The need to practice these exercises becomes even more apparent. In your reflecting and thinking time, you can confront that old negative trash, deliberately and clearly saying no. Calm down, quiet and receptive, and force yourself to hear good things about yourself.

Affirm yourself. Repeat those affirmations that tell you that you are God's beloved. Learn by reading scriptural passages and parables showing you that God loves you. When those old tapes start playing, telling you that if you were the lost sheep God would leave you to the wolves, confront that and tell yourself it simply is not valid. All of us must take the time, learn to be quiet, and listen to what is good about ourselves. When is your quiet time?

2. THINK

The mind is the door to spirituality, positive learning, the very door to God. We must dare to think, to use the gray matter God has given us. Asking ourselves, who is God to us, do we then tend to spout words we once learned? God is Jesus, God is Father, God is the Lamb of God, God is the Holy Spirit. Going beyond that, ask Who is God to me? Ask another question. What is the role of religion in my life? What is the power that I give religion over me? Does God really demand that I make no mistakes? Is God going to punish me or someone I love if I am not perfect? Who is God to me? Am I reacting to old messages rather than acting in the here and now? When we think and question these things, we may find that some of what we learned in the past was not wrong or bad. But until we really pause to reflect on it, we won't know whether we are acting on it because we choose to, or whether it is simply a value that was passed on to us. We can't know until we question and challenge.

Yes, challenge the old lessons! Challenge the old perceptions. When we take time to look back, we may agree with much of what we were taught. Marvelous! We keep it and it is ours forever. Ours because we choose it. That makes all the difference in the world! But when we make a god of religion and subsequently find that it is flawed, we may toss the whole thing out, God, spirituality, and all the strength and help that comes from a genuine, loving relationship with God—gone. Gone because we didn't take the time to sort it all out, to question, to challenge, to take the responsibility for what is ours and what is the truth.

Under the topic of "think," we must pay attention. God speaks to us hundreds of times a day, but we miss most of it. We don't pay attention to those angels, the messengers of God who appear throughout Scripture and throughout our lives. God's messengers can come in thousands of ways. In the rainfall. In the cool breeze. God can use the words of another person as a most powerful messenger. Maybe we have noticed a banner in church a thousand times, but have we truly seen it? Suddenly a light goes on and we really see that banner that says "Nowhere does God come closer to man than in man." Aha! Of course! We need to make Eucharist to one another, we need to be priest to one another. We see because we are finally paying attention! Opportunities for growth and drawing nearer to God are everywhere. But if we don't learn to think, if we don't learn to question, to challenge, to pay attention, we lose our avenue to God.

3. STUDY

There simply is no substitute for studying. All successful people know that they owe their success to being willing to do what other people won't do. It may be success in business, success in learning, success in building a spiritual life. Forego the effort, forego the fruit!

Studying can mean joining a class at church, learning about the intent and message in Scripture. There are always Bible classes available. If they have not appealed in the past because they were too fundamental, brainwashing, or whatever, study groups not connected to churches abound. Or self study—get hold of books and read. For years I have studied *The Dictionary of the Bible*, by John L. McKenzie. The author takes different themes from the Old Testament and ties them to the same theme in the New Testament, such as spirit, salvation, redemption, sin, love, sacrament, the word *Lord*, and the word *Gospel*. I wrote a whole book once on *God Seekers* basically inspired from a section in that book on spirit!

That kind of approach might not appeal to everyone. The main idea is to find some way to study under people who know more than we do. When we have learned to study, to reflect, to think, to understand, then we can internalize it, deepen it, make it our own.

4. READ SCRIPTURE

That idea is going to grate on some staunch, old-time Catholics like fingernails running down a blackboard. Why many of us were taught that reading Scripture was not permitted remains a mystery, but taught we were. This is no longer the case, but we have some catching up to do. We need to take the time to read and reflect on how God speaks to us through various passages and parables in the Bible.

I am constantly amazed and amused at how often Christ chose to work his miracles on the Sabbath. The Sabbath, of course, was a day when devout Jews did absolutely nothing but rest and pray. They could not ride on their donkeys, carry money in their pockets, or even light a fire. It would seem that Jesus went out of his way to annoy the Pharisees who sent a man to question Jesus. "Rabbi, if my ox falls in a pit and is hurt, am I allowed to draw it out on the Sabbath?" The trap was set. But Jesus' comments and actions, time and again, were specifically to rescue the beast, to heal on the Sabbath. Think on that, reflect on that. Ignoring the snare, Jesus said so clearly—the Sabbath was made for man, man was not made for the Sabbath.

We may have become modern-day Pharisees. Have we made religion, spirituality, the search for God so rigid, so much dead ritual, that it is no wonder we cannot find God in it? Through that passage about healing on the Sabbath, might God be speaking to us, telling us to let go of the past, the pain and resentment about that priest or nun or preacher? Is Scripture saying that the most important thing to God is a loving relationship with us, not scrupulous observance of the rules? Read, study, reflect, listen!

Take the time to search out passages that are meaningful and make them yours. In times of loneliness and hurt, or joy and celebration, those dog-eared pages will be there to turn to, to comfort you, to be a direct line of communication with God.

5. SHARE

"Joy not shared is cut in half, trouble not shared is doubled." That old saying is a perfect illustration of why sharing, going outside ourselves to another person, produces wisdom. If we keep everything inside, we invariably end up talking to ourselves, having only our own uncritical validation. Incessant hollow talking with others and never going inside ourselves is equally to be avoided. We are not talking about discussion groups, but faith-sharing about the unique way spirituality is active and effective in our lives. Always, such an exchange makes us more aware of the burning bush in our daily world, the beautiful ways in which God reaches out to us.

6. FIND A COMMUNITY

No one can develop healthy spirituality alone. On the other hand, no one can do it for us. We need other people around to keep who we are and what we are doing, real. Without community, we can dream up almost anything and think that it is of God. A community will challenge, open new doors, investigate, and affirm us when we are on course. Real meanings need to be ritualized. We ritualize two people's love for each other through matrimony, and the symbol of the wedding ring. Commitment to sobriety in Alcoholics Anonymous is often ritualized in the ceremony when medallions are given out symbolizing the passing of various lengths of sobriety—days, months, years. Meanings cry out to be ritualized. Without a community, how can we ritualize those significant events in our life? A community may or may not be officially "religious." It might be a "we care" group possibly found following a painful divorce. But once we have ceased to demand that religion be perfect, that professional religious people be beyond reproach, we may be able to return to our religion, this time retaining our power. Rather than an obstacle, it can be a tremendous help in our spiritual growth. What is your community?

7. USE CHECKS AND BALANCES

As we move toward spiritual independence, away from the pray, pay, obey posture we assumed in the past, we will be taking positive steps, even if they are sometimes baby steps, frequently reviewing our progress, checking up to see where we are. Have we regressed somewhere along the line, resuming old discarded values? Have we built our very own rituals? One helpful ritual used by many "Twelve-Step" people is to hold a burial service for hostility and resentment. Borrowing from them, get a little box, put into it some symbol of all that was bad in the past, and bury the critter. Pouring the dirt over it sets you free. Or, burn it. Write down the dreaded item—sin, fear, anger—and then (in a safe place, please) set it on fire. As it burns, the monster is taken away. You are freed. Without your own little rituals, sometimes that freedom just cannot be attained.

Consider now a six-point Bill of Rights for those of us pursuing a lively spirituality. Each right, of course, carries an equal responsibility.

1. We have a right to pursue God as best we know how, regardless of all those old false messages. Our responsibility is to study, pray, and discern, seriously seeking the truth.

2. We have a right to use our own minds in making decisions as to the nature of God and how God deals in human affairs. Our responsibility is to listen, remaining cognizant of the fact that God is greater than we are.

3. We have a right to make free decisions about the nature of religion and how much power we will give religion in our lives. Our responsibility is to live by the consequences of our decisions.

4. We have a right, if we choose religion, to expect to find in it genuine sources of aid and assistance for a robust spirituality. Our responsibility is to be realistic about the humanness of religion, not demanding perfection from it or its professional practitioners.

5. We have a right to experience the freeing, saving love of God. Our responsibility is to recover so that we can accept it as our own reality.

6. We have a right to choose the institutional church. Our responsibility is to have full knowledge of its past failures and promises.

Listen! God may very well be whispering, come, take communion with me. Bone of my bone. Flesh of my flesh. Blood of my blood. I am here because I am in love with you and I truly wish to have a deep, personal, intimate relationship with you. I am here, as open and vulnerable as I can be, and still you do not approach. Dearly beloved, I wait.

Fingerprint of God

Somehow, somewhere,
coded as deeply within our collective consciousness as the
desire to survive and multiply,
is the more that is home,
a home that is part of us and we part of it,
a place to go and belong.
Perhaps the inborn desire for growth that leads us home
is
the fingerprint of God, left as the last touch as we were
sent on our way—
a way that dents and terrifies us,
that challenges us to be, to become more whole, to find
the face of God and our own name in that finding.

Epilogue: A Meditation

Essentially, recovery is healing, and healing is human growth. Without the discipline and joy of meditation, however, we lose an extremely important method to quicken, enhance, and deepen that growth. The skill involved takes time and practice, but it is not so difficult that it is available only to a select, elite few.

Meditation falls under the category of "doing nothing," probably one of the reasons we don't persist long enough to incorporate it into our lives and reap the benefits. Most of us have been taught that to do nothing is to waste time. Wasting time makes us feel guilty. Putting meditation into the category of doing nothing hardly means it is useless, however. We can get into an emotional civil war with feelings of guilt and uselessness when we are not doing something productive, which makes it more important than ever to learn to practice meditation by sitting quietly and becoming very good at doing nothing.

Meditation gives us the mental discipline to live emotionally efficient lives. We learn how to do one thing at a time. How often are we preoccupied with three or four things at a time, no single one of them receiving our full attention? This starts a worry cycle—what has already happened, what might be happening now, what will happen in the future. Things pile up so fast we can't deal with them. Meditation helps us to stop wasting enormous amounts of energy running around and around in a squirrel cage of frantic, disconnected thoughts.

Through meditation we become more aware of our interior life. What does the inside of a beautiful day look like? What is the inside of a child's feelings on Christmas day? What is happening on the inside of the people and events that crowd around us? It is a whole new dimension.

Once we have mastered at least elementary meditation we have a safe place to go. We can retreat to this safety to deal with our broken spirits, our hurts and sins. No longer must we run away, wrecking our day, wrecking our week, wrecking our life. Now the world is not so terrifying. We are emotionally efficient and spiritually stable.

There are many ways to meditate. I have found the one I am about to describe to be very effective. It is simple. Practiced diligently, it becomes a tremendously powerful tool to improve sensitivity and awareness.

First you need to establish a state of being, so that you can easily and effortlessly "go to your state," meaning that you have put yourself into a proper environment removed from distractions, and have achieved a proper state of mind, thoroughly relaxed and at ease. By experimenting a bit, you can decide whether soft music in the background is helpful to block out extraneous noise, or whether you prefer silence. The point is to be relaxed and comfortable.

Second—breathe. Take at least four deep breaths. Breathe in, breathe out; breathe in, breathe out. Relax. Letting your mind forget any difficult problems, roll your head around, rolling it from side to side, relaxing your neck and shoulders. Relaxed, you become quiet. More deep breaths. Quieted down. Now image a door. To walk through it, you must put down all the packages you are carrying, one by one. Put down the package of worry. Leave it outside the door. Put down that heavy bundle of guilt, and that huge parcel of fear and frustration and anger. They are very real bundles that must be laid down. Put them down one by one, so you can walk freely through the door, your mind quiet.

You have become receptive, ready to listen actively. You are not going to sleep. You become ultra-conscious not unconscious. You are only listening to the words spoken within, the inner reality. You have withdrawn in order to gain strength and wisdom, not to think about pressing problems.

Once through the door, free of your burdensome packages, you mentally sit down in a chair that is waiting for you, you look back through the door which you entered. And you wait. Wait to see what will appear. You have no big objective, nothing to accomplish, it is a time to do nothing. You listen to who you are. You see the inner reality of all the wisdom around you. This is "going to your state."

Now image a very beautiful beach. You walk along that beach, feeling the white, warm sand under your feet, smelling the salt water, listening to the waves lap up on the beach, feeling the cool water as it swirls around your ankles. Listen to the seagulls, breathe in the salt air! It is comfortable. It is freeing. It is a wonderful place to be. But as you continue to walk, you begin to get tired. The sand begins to pull at your feet. It is harder and harder to lift your feet out of the sand. For some reason, you know that you must not stop walking. You must get to a certain place. It doesn't feel so wonderful any longer to walk along the beach. The water has gotten colder and the sand sucks harder at your feet. You are very fatigued. Desperately tired, realizing that you must continue, you become afraid. What if you can't complete the journey? Yet your inner voice says you must. Your legs hurt and a weight presses down on your shoulders. The beach is no longer a friendly place. You feel that weight. You feel the pain in your legs. It is harder and harder to breathe. It is all such hard work. Fear, fatigue, pain. All of a sudden, you know you are not going to be able to complete your journey. No more energy. No more strength. You must keep going—but you can't make it any longer. In that total fatigue, you suddenly sense the presence of someone walking beside you. It seems to be a friendly presence. Somehow amid all the pain and fatigue and worry, you sense that this person cares and is there to help; this person even loves you. Just when you think you simply cannot take another step, this person walking beside you reaches over, lifts you, and carries you. Your feet no longer hurt, your legs no longer hurt, your lungs no longer hurt. You are being carried. The journey no longer depends on you alone, on your strength. You are being carried, and you are afraid, because you have never been carried before. Everything has always been up to you. Until now, only your own strength counted.

Even though being carried is blissful, you say to the person carrying you, put me down, put me down! I don't trust you! You may stop carrying me and I am afraid you will drop me! Still resisting being loved in the quiet place in your spirit, you look up and see the face of the One who is carrying you. You look straight into infinite love, infinite strength, infinite understanding. Though no words are spoken, you hear that person saying to you, "Hush, be quiet, rest. Let me carry you for a while. I have strength enough for both of us. Be still. Be quiet. Be tamed. Trust that I will never let you fall." And you quietly, peacefully surrender to the love and strength of the Other. It feels so good. You let yourself be carried. From somewhere outside yourself you can look down upon this scene, watching this wonderful, strong, loving Person with great care, great respect, great tenderness carrying you. You feel so safe.

You see your inner reality, the limits of your own power, and the need we all have to be carried at times. You see the faith that there is One who will always carry you if you will only stop saying "Put me down." Finally, you allow that loving power to be sufficient unto you.

Suggestions for Further Reading

Bokenkotter, Thomas. *Essential Catholicism: Dynamics of Faith and Belief.* New York: Doubleday, 1986.

Greeley, Andrew, M. *Great Mysteries: An Essential Catechism.* rev. ed. San Francisco: Harper & Row, 1985.

Heschel, Abraham J. *Man's Quest for God: Studies in Prayer and Symbolism.* New York: Macmillan, 1981.

Wilhelm, Anthony. *Christ Among Us: A Modern Presentation of the Catholic Faith for Adults.* rev. ed. San Francisco: HarperCollins, 1990.